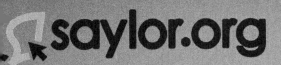

Information Systems for
Business and Beyond

D T. BOURGEOIS, PH.D.

SHED THROUGH THE OPEN TEXT BOOK CHALLENGE BY THE SAYLOR ACADEMY
ARY 2014

Information Systems for Business and Beyond

David T. Bourgeois, Ph.D.

Textbook Equity Edition

ISBN 978-1-304-94348-4

Contents

Introduction

Welcome to *Information Systems for Business and Beyond.* In this book, you will be introduced to the concept of information systems, their use in business, and the larger impact they are having on our world.

Audience

This book is written as an introductory text, meant for those with little or no experience with computers or information systems. While sometimes the descriptions can get a little bit technical, every effort has been made to convey the information essential to understanding a topic while not getting bogged down in detailed terminology or esoteric discussions.

Chapter Outline

The text is organized around thirteen chapters divided into three major parts, as follows:

- **Part 1: What Is an Information System?**
    - *Chapter 1: What Is an Information System?* – This chapter provides an overview of information systems, including the history of how we got where we are today.
    - *Chapter 2: Hardware* – We discuss information systems hardware and how it works. You will look at different computer parts and learn how they interact.
    - *Chapter 3: Software* – Without software, hardware is useless. In this chapter, we discuss software and the role it plays in an organization.
    - *Chapter 4: Data and Databases* – This chapter explores how organizations use information systems to turn data into information that can then be used for competitive advantage. Special attention is paid to the role of databases.
    - *Chapter 5: Networking and Communication* – Today's computers are expected to also be communication devices. In this chapter we review the history of networking, how the Internet works, and the use of networks in organizations today.
    - *Chapter 6: Information Systems Security* – We discuss the information security triad of confidentiality, integrity, and availability. We will review different security technologies, and the chapter concludes with a primer on personal information security.
- **Part 2: Information Systems for Strategic Advantage**
    - *Chapter 7: Does IT Matter?* – This chapter examines the impact that information systems have on an organization. Can IT give a company a competitive advantage? We will

discuss seminal works by Brynjolfsson, Carr, and Porter as they relate to IT and competitive advantage.

- *Chapter 8: Business Processes* – Business processes are the essence of what a business does, and information systems play an important role in making them work. This chapter will discuss business process management, business process reengineering, and ERP systems.

- *Chapter 9: The People in Information Systems* – This chapter will provide an overview of the different types of people involved in information systems. This includes people who create information systems, those who operate and administer information systems, those who manage information systems, and those who use information systems.

- *Chapter 10: Information Systems Development* – How are information systems created? This chapter will review the concept of programming, look at different methods of software development, review website and mobile application development, discuss end-user computing, and look at the "build vs. buy" decision that many companies face.

- *Part 3: Information Systems beyond the Organization*
  - *Chapter 11: Globalization and the Digital Divide* – The rapid rise of the Internet has made it easier than ever to do business worldwide. This chapter will look at the impact that the Internet is having on the globalization of business and the issues that firms must face because of it. It will also cover the concept of the digital divide and some of the steps being taken to alleviate it.

  - *Chapter 12: The Ethical and Legal Implications of Information Systems* – The rapid changes in information and communication technology in the past few decades have brought a broad array of new capabilities and powers to governments, organizations, and individuals alike. This chapter will discuss the effects that these new capabilities have had and the legal and regulatory changes that have been put in place in response.

  - *Chapter 13: Future Trends in Information Systems* – This final chapter will present an overview of some of the new technologies that are on the horizon. From wearable technology to 3-D printing, this chapter will provide a look forward to what the next few years will bring.

For the Student

Each chapter in this text begins with a list of the relevant learning objectives and ends with a chapter summary. Following the summary is a list of study questions that highlight key topics in the chapter. In order to get the best learning experience, you would be wise to begin by reading both the learning objectives and the summary and then reviewing the questions at the end of the chapter.

For the Instructor

Learning objectives can be found at the beginning of each chapter. Of course, all chapters are recommended for use in an introductory information systems course. However, for courses on a shorter calendar or courses using additional textbooks, a review of the learning objectives will help determine which chapters can be omitted.

At the end of each chapter, there is a set of study questions and exercises (except for chapter 1, which only offers study questions). The study questions can be assigned to help focus students' reading on the learning objectives. The exercises are meant to be a more in-depth, experiential way for students to learn chapter topics. It is recommended that you review any exercise before assigning it, adding any detail needed (such as length, due date) to complete the assignment.

Part 1: What Is an Information System?

Chapter 1: What Is an Information System?

Learning Objectives

Upon successful completion of this chapter, you will be able to:

- define what an information system is by identifying its major components;
- describe the basic history of information systems; and
- describe the basic argument behind the article "Does IT Matter?" by Nicholas Carr.

Introduction

If you are reading this, you are most likely taking a course in information systems, but do you even know what the course is going to cover? When you tell your friends or your family that you are taking a course in information systems, can you explain what it is about? For the past several years, I have taught an Introduction to Information Systems course. The first day of class I ask my students to tell me what they think an information system is. I generally get answers such as "computers," "databases," or "Excel." These are good answers, but definitely incomplete ones. The study of information systems goes far beyond understanding some technologies. Let's begin our study by defining information systems.

Defining Information Systems

Almost all programs in business require students to take a course in something called *information systems*. But what exactly does that term mean? Let's take a look at some of the more popular definitions, first from Wikipedia and then from a couple of textbooks:

- "Information systems (IS) is the study of complementary networks of hardware and software that people and organizations use to collect, filter, process, create, and distribute data."[1]
- "Information systems are combinations of hardware, software, and telecommunications networks that people build and use to collect, create, and distribute useful data, typically in organizational settings."[2]
- "Information systems are interrelated components working together to collect, process, store, and disseminate information to support decision making, coordination, control, analysis, and viualization in an organization."[3]

---

1. Wikipedia entry on "Information Systems," as displayed on August 19, 2012. *Wikipedia: The Free Encyclopedia*. San Francisco: Wikimedia Foundation. http://en.wikipedia.org/wiki/Information_systems_(discipline).
2. Excerpted from *Information Systems Today - Managing in the Digital World*, fourth edition. Prentice-Hall, 2010.
3. Excerpted from *Management Information Systems*, twelfth edition, Prentice-Hall, 2012.

As you can see, these definitions focus on two different ways of describing information systems: the _components_ that make up an information system and the _role_ that those components play in an organization. Let's take a look at each of these.

The Components of Information Systems

[handwritten annotation: (5) hardware, software, data, people, process]

As I stated earlier, I spend the first day of my information systems class discussing exactly what the term means. Many students understand that an information system has something to do with databases or spreadsheets. Others mention computers and e-commerce. And they are all right, at least in part: information systems are made up of different components that work together to provide value to an organization.

The first way I describe information systems to students is to tell them that they are made up of five components: hardware, software, data, people, and process. The first three, fitting under the category _technology_, are generally what most students think of when asked to define information systems. But the last two, people and process, are really what separate the idea of information systems from more technical fields, such as computer science. In order to fully understand information systems, students must understand how all of these components work together to bring value to an organization.

Technology

Technology can be thought of as the application of scientific knowledge for practical purposes. From the invention of the wheel to the harnessing of electricity for artificial lighting, technology is a part of our lives in so many ways that we tend to take it for granted. As discussed before, the first three components of information systems – hardware, software, and data – all fall under the category of technology. Each of these will get its own chapter and a much lengthier discussion, but we will take a moment here to introduce them so we can get a full understanding of what an information system is.

Hardware

Information systems hardware is the part of an information system you can touch – the physical components of the technology. Computers, keyboards, disk drives, iPads, and flash drives are all examples of information systems hardware. We will spend some time going over these components and how they all work together in chapter 2.

Software

Software is a set of instructions that tells the hardware what to do. Software is not tangible – it cannot be touched. When programmers create software programs, what they are really doing is simply typing out lists of instructions that tell the hardware what to do. There are several categories of software, with the two main categories being operating-system software, which makes the hardware usable, and application software, which does something useful. Examples of operating systems include Microsoft Windows on a personal computer and Google's Android on a mobile phone. Examples of application software are Microsoft Excel and Angry Birds. Software will be explored more thoroughly in chapter 3.

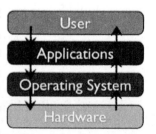

Data

The third component is data. You can think of data as a collection of facts. For example, your street address, the city you live in, and your phone number are all pieces of data. Like software, data is also intangible. By themselves, pieces of data are not really very useful. But aggregated, indexed, and organized together into a database, data can become a powerful tool for businesses. In fact, all of the definitions presented at the beginning of this chapter focused on how information systems manage data. Organizations collect all kinds of data and use it to make decisions. These decisions can then be analyzed as to their effectiveness and the organization can be improved. Chapter 4 will focus on data and databases, and their uses in organizations.

Networking Communication: A Fourth Technology Piece?

Besides the components of hardware, software, and data, which have long been considered the core technology of information systems, it has been suggested that one other component should be added: communication. An information system can exist without the ability to communicate – the first personal computers were stand-alone machines that did not access the Internet. However, in today's hyper-connected world, it is an extremely rare computer that does not connect to another device or to a network. Technically, the networking communication component is made up of hardware and software, but it is such a core feature of today's information systems that it has become its own category. We will be covering networking in chapter 5.

People – Systems analyst programmers

When thinking about information systems, it is easy to get focused on the technology components and forget that we must look beyond these tools to fully understand how they integrate into an organization. A focus on the people involved in information systems is the next step. From the front-line help-desk workers, to systems analysts, to programmers, all the way up to the chief information officer (CIO), the people involved with information systems are an essential element that must not be overlooked. The people component will be covered in chapter 9.

Process

The last component of information systems is process. A process is a series of steps undertaken to achieve a desired outcome or goal. Information systems are becoming more and more integrated with organizational processes, bringing more productivity and better control to those processes. But simply automating activities using technology is not enough – businesses looking to effectively utilize information systems do more. Using technology to manage and improve processes, both within a company and externally with suppliers and customers, is the ultimate goal. Technology buzzwords such as "business process reengineering," "business process management," and "enterprise resource planning" all have to do with the continued improvement of these business procedures and the integration of technology with them. Businesses hoping to gain an advantage over their competitors are highly focused on this component of information systems. We will discuss processes in chapter 8.

The Role of Information Systems

Now that we have explored the different components of information systems, we need to turn our attention to the role that information systems play in an organization. So far we have looked at what the components of an information system are, but what do these components actually do for an organization? From our definitions above, we see that these components collect, store, organize, and distribute data throughout the organization. In fact, we might say that one of the roles of information systems is to take data and turn it into information, and then transform that into organizational knowledge. As technology has developed, this role has evolved into the backbone of the organization. To get a full appreciation of the role information systems play, we will review how they have changed over the years.

IBM 704 Mainframe (Copyright: Lawrence Livermore National Laboratory)

The Mainframe Era

From the late 1950s through the 1960s, computers were seen as a way to more efficiently do calculations. These first business computers were room-sized monsters, with several refrigerator-sized machines linked together. The primary work of these devices was to organize and store large volumes of information that were tedious to manage by hand. Only large businesses, universities, and government agencies could afford them, and they took a crew of specialized personnel and specialized facilities to maintain. These devices served dozens to hundreds of users at a time through a process called time-sharing. Typical functions included scientific calculations and accounting, under the broader umbrella of "data processing."

In the late 1960s, the Manufacturing Resources Planning (MRP) systems were introduced. This software, running on a mainframe computer, gave companies the ability to manage the manufacturing process, making it more efficient. From tracking inventory to creating bills of materials to scheduling production, the MRP systems (and later the MRP II systems) gave more businesses a reason to want to integrate computing into their processes. IBM became the dominant mainframe company. Nicknamed

Registered trademark of International Business Machines

"Big Blue," the company became synonymous with business computing. Continued improvement in software and the availability of cheaper hardware eventually brought mainframe computers (and their little sibling, the minicomputer) into most large businesses.

The PC Revolution

In 1975, the first microcomputer was announced on the cover of *Popular Mechanics*: the Altair 8800. Its immediate popularity sparked the imagination of entrepreneurs everywhere, and there were quickly dozens of companies making these "personal computers." Though at first just a niche product for computer hobbyists, improvements in usability and the availability of practical software led to growing sales. The most prominent of these early personal computer makers was a little company known as Apple Computer, headed by Steve Jobs and Steve Wozniak, with the hugely successful "Apple II." Not wanting to be left out of the revolution, in 1981 IBM (teaming with a little company called Microsoft for their operating-system software) hurriedly released their own version of the personal computer, simply called the "PC." Businesses, who had used IBM mainframes for years to run their businesses, finally had the permission they needed to bring personal computers into their companies, and the IBM PC took off. The IBM PC was named *Time* magazine's "Man of the Year" for 1982.

Because of the IBM PC's open architecture, it was easy for other companies to copy, or "clone" it. During the 1980s, many new computer companies sprang up, offering less expensive versions of the PC. This drove prices down and spurred innovation. Microsoft developed its Windows operating system and made the PC even easier to use. Common uses for the PC during this period included word processing, spreadsheets, and databases. These early PCs were not connected to any sort of network; for the most part they stood alone as islands of innovation within the larger organization.

Client-Server

In the mid-1980s, businesses began to see the need to connect their computers together as a way to collaborate and share resources. This networking architecture was referred to as "client-server" because users would log in to the local area network (LAN) from their PC (the "client") by connecting to a powerful computer called a "server," which would then grant them rights to different resources on the network (such as shared file areas and a printer). Software companies began developing applications that allowed multiple users to access the same data at the same time. This evolved into software applications for communicating, with the first real popular use of electronic mail appearing at this time.

Registered trademark of SAP

This networking and data sharing all stayed within the confines of each business, for the most part. While there was sharing of electronic data between companies, this was a very specialized function. Computers were now seen as tools to collaborate internally, within an organization. In fact, these networks of computers were becoming so powerful that they were replacing many of the functions previously performed by the larger mainframe computers at a fraction of the cost. It was during this era that the first Enterprise Resource Planning (ERP) systems were developed and run on the client-server architecture. An ERP system is a software application with a centralized database that can be used to run a company's entire business. With separate modules for accounting, finance, inventory, human resources, and many, many more, ERP systems, with Germany's SAP leading the way, represented the state of the art in information systems integration. We will discuss ERP systems as part of the chapter on process (chapter 9).

The World Wide Web and E-Commerce

First invented in 1969, the Internet was confined to use by universities, government agencies, and researchers for many years. Its rather arcane commands and user applications made it unsuitable for mainstream use in business. One exception to this was the ability to expand electronic mail outside the confines of a single organization. While the first e-mail messages on the Internet were sent in the early 1970s, companies who wanted to expand their LAN-based e-mail started hooking up to the Internet in the 1980s. Companies began connecting their internal networks to the Internet in order to allow communication between their employees and employees at other companies. It was with these early Internet connections that the computer truly began to evolve from a computational device to a communications device.

In 1989, Tim Berners-Lee developed a simpler way for researchers to share information over the network at CERN laboratories, a concept he called the World Wide Web.[4] This invention became the launching point of the growth of the Internet as a way for businesses to share information about themselves.

As web browsers and Internet connections became the norm, companies rushed to grab domain names and create websites.

In 1991, the National Science Foundation, which governed how the Internet was used, lifted restrictions on its commercial use. The year 1994 saw the establishment of both eBay and Amazon.com, two true pioneers in the use of the new digital marketplace. A mad rush of investment in Internet-based businesses led to the dot-com boom through the late 1990s,

amazon.com®

Registered trademark of Amazon Technologies, Inc.

and then the dot-com bust in 2000. While much can be learned from the speculation and crazy economic theories espoused during that bubble, one important outcome for businesses was that thousands of miles of Internet connections were laid around the world during that time. The world became truly "wired" heading into the new millenium, ushering in the era of globalization, which we will discuss in chapter 11.

As it became more expected for companies to be connected to the Internet, the digital world also became a more dangerous place. Computer viruses and worms, once slowly propagated through the sharing of computer disks, could now grow with tremendous speed via the Internet. Software written for a disconnected world found it very difficult to defend against these sorts of threats. A whole new industry of computer and Internet security arose. We will study information security in chapter 6.

Web 2.0

As the world recovered from the dot-com bust, the use of technology in business continued to evolve at a frantic pace. Websites became interactive; instead of just visiting a site to find out about a business and purchase its products, customers wanted to be able to customize their experience and interact with the business. This new type of interactive website, where you did not have to know how to create a web page or do any programming in order to put information online, became known as web 2.0. Web 2.0 is exemplified by blogging, social networking, and interactive comments being available on many websites. This new web-2.0 world, in which online interaction became expected, had a big impact on many businesses and even whole industries. Some industries, such as bookstores, found themselves relegated to a niche status. Others, such as video rental chains and travel agencies, simply began going out of business as they were replaced by online technologies. This process of technology replacing a middleman in a transaction is called disintermediation.

As the world became more connected, new questions arose. Should access to the Internet be considered a right? Can I copy a song that I downloaded from the Internet? How can I keep information that I have put on a website private? What information is acceptable to collect from children? Technology moved so fast that policymakers did not have enough time to enact appropriate laws, making for a Wild West–type atmosphere. Ethical issues surrounding information systems will be covered in chapter 12.

The Post-PC World

After thirty years as the primary computing device used in most businesses, sales of the PC are now beginning to decline as sales of tablets and smartphones are taking off. Just as the mainframe before it, the PC will continue to play a key role in business, but will no longer be the primary way that people interact and do business. The limited storage and processing power of these devices is being offset by a move to "cloud" computing, which allows for storage, sharing, and backup of information on a massive scale. This

---

4. CERN's "The Birth of the Web." http://public.web.cern.ch/public/en/about/web-en.html

will require new rounds of thinking and innovation on the part of businesses as technology continues to advance.

The

Eras of Business Computing

Era	Hardware	Operating System	Applications
Mainframe (1970s)	Terminals connected to mainframe computer.	Time-sharing (TSO) on MVS	Custom-written MRP software
PC (mid-1980s)	IBM PC or compatible. Sometimes connected to mainframe computer via expansion card.	MS-DOS	WordPerfect, Lotus 1-2-3
Client-Server (late 80s to early 90s)	IBM PC "clone" on a Novell Network.	Windows for Workgroups	Microsoft Word, Microsoft Excel
World Wide Web (mid-90s to early 2000s)	IBM PC "clone" connected to company intranet.	Windows XP	Microsoft Office, Internet Explorer
Web 2.0 (mid-2000s to present)	Laptop connected to company Wi-Fi.	Windows 7	Microsoft Office, Firefox
Post-PC (today and beyond)	Apple iPad	iOS	Mobile-friendly websites, mobile apps

Can Information Systems Bring Competitive Advantage?

It has always been the assumption that the implementation of information systems will, in and of itself, bring a business competitive advantage. After all, if installing one computer to manage inventory can make a company more efficient, won't installing several computers to handle even more of the business continue to improve it?

In 2003, Nicholas Carr wrote an article in the *Harvard Business Review* that questioned this assumption. The article, entitled "IT Doesn't Matter," raised the idea that information technology has become just a commodity. Instead of viewing technology as an investment that will make a company stand out, it should be seen as something like electricity: It should be managed to reduce costs, ensure that it is always running, and be as risk-free as possible.

As you might imagine, this article was both hailed and scorned. Can IT bring a competitive advantage? It sure did for Walmart (see sidebar). We will discuss this topic further in chapter 7.

Sidebar: Walmart Uses Information Systems to Become the World's Leading Retailer

Walmart is the world's largest retailer, earning $15.2 billion on sales of $443.9 billion in the fiscal year that ended on January 31, 2012. Walmart currently serves over 200 million customers every week, worldwide.[5] Walmart's rise to prominence is due in no small part to their use of information systems.

Registered trademark of Wal-Mart Stores, Inc.

One of the keys to this success was the implementation of Retail Link, a supply-chain management system. This system, unique when initially implemented in the mid-1980s, allowed Walmart's suppliers to directly access the inventory levels and sales information of their products at any of Walmart's more than ten thousand stores. Using Retail Link, suppliers can analyze how well their products are selling at one or more Walmart stores, with a range of reporting options. Further, Walmart requires the suppliers to use Retail Link to manage their own inventory levels. If a supplier feels that their products are selling out too quickly, they can use Retail Link to petition Walmart to raise the levels of inventory for their products. This has essentially allowed Walmart to "hire" thousands of product managers, all of whom have a vested interest in the products they are managing. This revolutionary approach to managing inventory has allowed Walmart to continue to drive prices down and respond to market forces quickly.

Today, Walmart continues to innovate with information technology. Using its tremendous market presence, any technology that Walmart requires its suppliers to implement immediately becomes a business standard.

Summary

In this chapter, you have been introduced to the concept of information systems. We have reviewed several definitions, with a focus on the components of information systems: technology, people, and process. We have reviewed how the business use of information systems has evolved over the years, from the use of large mainframe computers for number crunching, through the introduction of the PC and networks, all the way to the era of mobile computing. During each of these phases, new innovations in software and technology allowed businesses to integrate technology more deeply.

We are now to a point where every company is using information systems and asking the question: Does it bring a competitive advantage? In the end, that is really what this book is about. Every businessperson should understand what an information system is and how it can be used to bring a competitive advantage. And that is the task we have before us.

Study Questions

1. What are the five components that make up an information system?
2. What are three examples of information system hardware?

5. Walmart 2012 Annual Report.

3. Microsoft Windows is an example of which component of information systems?

4. What is application software?

5. What roles do people play in information systems?

6. What is the definition of a process?

7. What was invented first, the personal computer or the Internet (ARPANET)?

8. In what year were restrictions on commercial use of the Internet first lifted? When were eBay and Amazon founded?

9. What does it mean to say we are in a "post-PC world"?

10. What is Carr's main argument about information technology?

Exercises

1. Suppose that you had to explain to a member of your family or one of your closest friends the concept of an information system. How would you define it? Write a one-paragraph description *in your own words* that you feel would best describe an information system to your friends or family.

2. Of the five primary components of an information system (hardware, software, data, people, process), which do you think is the most important to the success of a business organization? Write a one-paragraph answer to this question that includes an example from your personal experience to support your answer.

3. We all interact with various information systems every day: at the grocery store, at work, at school, even in our cars (at least some of us). Make a list of the different information systems you interact with every day. See if you can identify the technologies, people, and processes involved in making these systems work.

4. Do you agree that we are in a post-PC stage in the evolution of information systems? Some people argue that we will always need the personal computer, but that it will not be the primary device used for manipulating information. Others think that a whole new era of mobile and biological computing is coming. Do some original research and make your prediction about what business computing will look like in the next generation.

5. The Walmart case study introduced you to how that company used information systems to become the world's leading retailer. Walmart has continued to innovate and is still looked to as a leader in the use of technology. Do some original research and write a one-page report detailing a new technology that Walmart has recently implemented or is pioneering.

Chapter 2: Hardware

Learning Objectives

Upon successful completion of this chapter, you will be able to:

- describe information systems hardware;
- identify the primary components of a computer and the functions they perform; and
- explain the effect of the commoditization of the personal computer.

Introduction

As we learned in the first chapter, an information system is made up of five components: hardware, software, data, people, and process. The physical parts of computing devices – those that you can actually touch – are referred to as hardware. In this chapter, we will take a look at this component of information systems, learn a little bit about how it works, and discuss some of the current trends surrounding it.

As stated above, computer hardware encompasses digital devices that you can physically touch. This includes devices such as the following:

- desktop computers
- laptop computers
- mobile phones
- tablet computers
- e-readers
- storage devices, such as flash drives
- input devices, such as keyboards, mice, and scanners
- output devices such as printers and speakers.

Besides these more traditional computer hardware devices, many items that were once not considered digital devices are now becoming computerized themselves. Digital technologies are now being integrated into many everyday objects, so the days of a device being labeled categorically as computer hardware may be ending. Examples of these types of digital devices include automobiles, refrigerators, and even soft-drink dispensers. In this chapter, we will also explore digital devices, beginning with defining what we mean by the term itself.

Digital Devices

Assembler Process

A digital device processes electronic signals that represent either a one ("on") or a zero ("off"). The *on* state is represented by the presence of an electronic signal; the *off* state is represented by the absence of an electronic signal. Each one or zero is referred to as a *bit* (a contraction of *binary digit*); a group of eight bits is a *byte*. The first personal computers could process 8 bits of data at once; modern PCs can now process 64 bits of data at a time, which is where the term *64-bit processor* comes from.

Sidebar: Understanding Binary

As you know, the system of numbering we are most familiar with is base-ten numbering. In base-ten numbering, each column in the number represents a power of ten, with the far-right column representing 10^0 (ones), the next column from the right representing 10^1 (tens), then 10^2 (hundreds), then 10^3 (thousands), etc. For example, the number 1010 in decimal represents: (1 x 1000) + (0 x 100) + (1 x 10) + (0 x 1).

Computers use the base-two numbering system, also known as binary. In this system, each column in the number represents a power of two, with the far-right column representing 2^0 (ones), the next column from the right representing 2^1 (tens), then 2^2 (fours), then 2^3 (eights), etc. For example, the number 1010 in binary represents (1 x 8) + (0 x 4) + (1 x 2) + (0 x 1). In base ten, this evaluates to 10.

As the capacities of digital devices grew, new terms were developed to identify the capacities of processors, memory, and disk storage space. Prefixes were applied to the word *byte* to represent different orders of magnitude. Since these are digital specifications, the prefixes were originally meant to represent multiples of 1024 (which is 2^{10}), but have more recently been rounded to mean multiples of 1000.

A Listing of Binary Prefixes

Prefix	Represents	Example
kilo	one thousand	kilobyte=one thousand bytes
mega	one million	megabyte=one million bytes
giga	one billion	gigabyte=one billion bytes
tera	one trillion	terabyte=one trillion bytes

Tour of a PC

All personal computers consist of the same basic components: a CPU, memory, circuit board, storage, and input/output devices. It also turns out that almost every digital device uses the same set of components, so examining the personal computer will give us insight into the structure of a variety of digital devices. So let's take a "tour" of a personal computer and see what makes them function.

Processing Data: The CPU — *designed by experts in Boolean Logic*

As stated above, most computing devices have a similar architecture. The core of this architecture is the central processing unit, or CPU. The CPU can be thought of as the "brains" of the device. The CPU carries out the commands sent to it by the software and returns results to be acted upon.

The earliest CPUs were large circuit boards with limited functionality. Today, a CPU is generally on one chip and can perform a large variety of functions. There are two primary manufacturers of CPUs for personal computers: Intel and Advanced Micro Devices (AMD).

The speed ("clock time") of a CPU is measured in hertz. A hertz is defined as one cycle per second. Using the binary prefixes mentioned above, we can see that a kilohertz (abbreviated kHz) is one thousand cycles per second, a megahertz (mHz) is one million cycles per second, and a gigahertz (gHz) is one billion cycles per second. The CPU's processing power is increasing at an amazing rate (see the sidebar about Moore's Law). Besides a faster clock time, many CPU chips now contain multiple processors per chip. These chips, known as dual-core (two processors) or quad-core (four processors), increase the processing power of a computer by providing the capability of multiple CPUs.

Sidebar: Moore's Law

We all know that computers get faster every year. Many times, we are not sure if we want to buy today's model of smartphone, tablet, or PC because next week it won't be the most advanced any more. Gordon Moore, one of the founders of Intel, recognized this phenomenon in 1965, noting that microprocessor transistor counts had been doubling every year.[1] His insight eventually evolved into Moore's Law, which states that the number of transistors on a chip will double every two years. This has been generalized into the concept that computing power will double every two years for the same price point. Another way of looking at this is to think that the price for the same computing power will be cut in half every two years. Though many have predicted its demise, Moore's Law has held true for over forty years (see figure below).

Analog Computer - uses a measurable factor to represent specific data.

---

[1]. Moore, Gordon E. (1965). "Cramming more components onto integrated circuits" (PDF). Electronics Magazine. p. 4. Retrieved 2012-10-18.

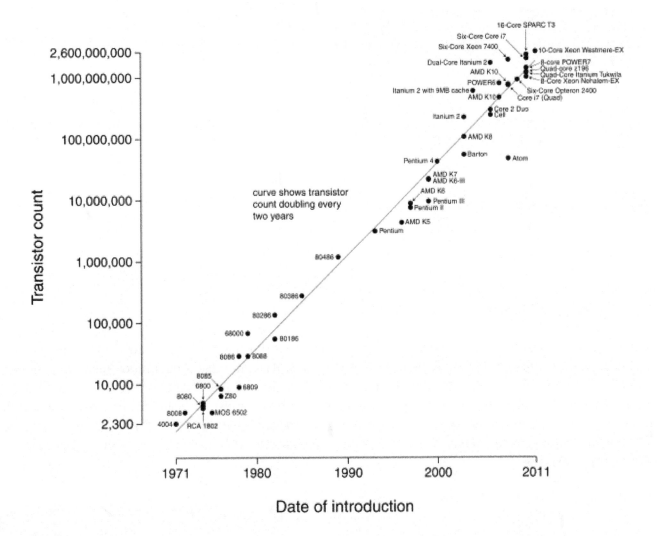

A graphical representation of Moore's Law (CC-BY-SA: Wgsimon)

There will be a point, someday, where we reach the limits of Moore's Law, where we cannot continue to shrink circuits any further. But engineers will continue to seek ways to increase performance.

Motherboard 2.3 - 2.4

Motherboard (click image to enlarge)

The motherboard is the main circuit board on the computer. The CPU, memory, and storage components, among other things, all connect into the motherboard. Motherboards come in different shapes and sizes, depending upon how compact or expandable the computer is designed to be. Most modern motherboards have many integrated components, such as video and sound processing, which used to require separate components.

The motherboard provides much of the bus of the computer (the term *bus* refers to the electrical connection between different computer components). The bus is an important determiner of the computer's speed: the combination of how fast the bus can transfer data and the number of data bits that can be moved at one time determine the speed.

Random-Access Memory

When a computer starts up, it begins to load information from the hard disk into its working memory. This working memory, called random-access memory (RAM), can transfer data much faster than the hard disk. Any program that you are running on the computer is loaded into RAM for processing. In order for a computer to work effectively, some minimal amount of RAM must be installed. In most cases, adding more RAM will allow the computer to run faster. Another characteristic of RAM is that it is "volatile." This means that it can store data as long as it is receiving power; when the computer is turned off, any data stored in RAM is lost.

RAM is generally installed in a personal computer through the use of a dual-inline memory module (DIMM). The type of DIMM accepted into a computer is dependent upon the motherboard. As described by Moore's Law, the amount of memory and speeds of DIMMs have increased dramatically over the years.

Memory DIMM (click image to enlarge)

Hard Disk

While the RAM is used as working memory, the computer also needs a place to store data for the longer term. Most of today's personal computers use a hard disk for long-term data storage. A hard disk is where data is stored when the computer is turned off and where it is retrieved from when the computer is turned on. Why is it called a hard disk? A hard disk consists of a stack of disks inside a hard metal case. A floppy disk (discussed below) was a removable disk that, in some cases at least, was flexible, or "floppy."

Hard disk enclosure (click image to enlarge)

Solid-State Drives

A relatively new component becoming more common in some personal computers is the solid-state drive (SSD). The SSD performs the same function as a hard disk: long-term storage. Instead of spinning disks, the SSD uses flash memory, which is much faster.

Solid-state drives are currently quite a bit more expensive than hard disks. However, the use of flash memory instead of disks makes them much lighter and faster than hard disks. SSDs are primarily utilized in portable computers, making them lighter and more efficient. Some computers combine the two storage technologies, using the SSD for the most accessed data (such as the operating system) while using the hard disk for data that is accessed less frequently. As with any technology, Moore's Law is driving up capacity and speed and lowering prices of solid-state drives, which will allow them to proliferate in the years to come.

Removable Media

Besides fixed storage components, removable storage media are also used in most personal computers. Removable media allows you to take your data with you. And just as with all other digital technologies, these media have gotten smaller and more powerful as the years have gone by. Early computers used floppy disks, which could be inserted into a disk drive in the computer. Data was stored on a magnetic disk inside an enclosure. These disks ranged from 8″ in the earliest days down to 3 1/2″.

Floppy-disk evolution (8″ to 5 1/4″ to 3 1/2″) (Public Domain)

Around the turn of the century, a new portable storage technology was being developed: the USB flash drive (more about the USB port later in the chapter). This device attaches to the universal serial bus (USB) connector, which became standard on all personal computers beginning in the late 1990s. As with all other storage media, flash drive storage capacity has skyrocketed over the years, from initial capacities of eight megabytes to current capacities of 64 gigabytes and still growing.

Network Connection

When personal computers were first developed, they were stand-alone units, which meant that data was brought into the computer or removed from the computer via removable media, such as the floppy disk. Beginning in the mid-1980s, however, organizations began to see the value in connecting computers together via a digital network. Because of this, personal computers needed the ability to connect to these networks. Initially, this was done by adding an expansion card to the computer that enabled the network connection, but by the mid-1990s, a network port was standard on most personal computers. As wireless technologies began to dominate in the early 2000s, many personal computers also began including wireless networking capabilities. Digital communication technologies will be discussed further in chapter 5.

Input and Output

USB connector (click image to enlarge)

In order for a personal computer to be useful, it must have channels for receiving input from the user and channels for delivering output to the user. These input and output devices connect to the computer via various connection ports, which generally are part of the motherboard and are accessible outside the computer case. In early personal computers, specific ports were designed for each type of output device. The configuration of these ports has evolved over the years, becoming more and more standardized over time. Today, almost all devices plug into a computer through the use of a USB port. This port type, first introduced in 1996, has increased in its capabilities, both in its data transfer rate and power supplied.

Bluetooth

Besides USB, some input and output devices connect to the computer via a wireless-technology standard called Bluetooth. Bluetooth was first invented in the 1990s and exchanges data over short distances using radio waves. Bluetooth generally has a range of 100 to 150 feet. For devices to communicate via Bluetooth, both the personal computer and the connecting device must have a Bluetooth communication chip installed.

Input Devices

All personal computers need components that allow the user to input data. Early computers used simply a keyboard to allow the user to enter data or select an item from a menu to run a program. With the advent of the graphical user interface, the mouse became a standard component of a computer. These two components are still the primary input devices to a personal computer, though variations of each have been introduced with varying levels of success over the years. For example, many new devices now use a touch screen as the primary way of entering data.

Besides the keyboard and mouse, additional input devices are becoming more common. Scanners allow users to input documents into a computer, either as images or as text. Microphones can be used to record audio or give voice commands. Webcams and other types of video cameras can be used to record video or participate in a video chat session.

Output Devices

Output devices are essential as well. The most obvious output device is a display, visually representing the state of the computer. In some cases, a personal computer can support multiple displays or be connected to larger-format displays such as a projector or large-screen television. Besides displays, other output devices include speakers for audio output and printers for printed output.

Sidebar: What Hardware Components Contribute to the Speed of My Computer?

The speed of a computer is determined by many elements, some related to hardware and some related to software. In hardware, speed is improved by giving the electrons shorter distances to traverse to complete a circuit. Since the first CPU was created in the early 1970s, engineers have constantly worked to figure out how to shrink these circuits and put more and more circuits onto the same chip. And this work has paid off – the speed of computing devices has been continuously improving ever since.

The hardware components that contribute to the speed of a personal computer are the CPU, the motherboard, RAM, and the hard disk. In most cases, these items can be replaced with newer, faster components. In the case of RAM, simply adding more RAM can also speed up the computer. The table below shows how each of these contributes to the speed of a computer. Besides upgrading hardware, there are many changes that can be made to the software of a computer to make it faster.

Component	Speed measured by	Units	Description
CPU	Clock speed	gHz	The time it takes to complete a circuit.
Motherboard	Bus speed	mHz	How much data can move across the bus simultaneously.
RAM	Data transfer rate	MB/s	The time it takes for data to be transferred from memory to system.
Hard Disk	Access time	ms	The time it takes before the disk can transfer data.
	Data transfer rate	MBit/s	The time it takes for data to be transferred from disk to system.

Other Computing Devices

A personal computer is designed to be a general-purpose device. That is, it can be used to solve many different types of problems. As the technologies of the personal computer have become more commonplace, many of the components have been integrated into other devices that previously were purely mechanical. We have also seen an evolution in what defines a computer. Ever since the invention of the personal computer, users have clamored for a way to carry them around. Here we will examine several types of devices that represent the latest trends in personal computing.

Portable Computers

A modern laptop

In 1983, Compaq Computer Corporation developed the first commercially successful portable personal computer. By today's standards, the Compaq PC was not very portable: weighing in at 28 pounds, this computer was portable only in the most literal sense – it could be carried around. But this was no laptop; the computer was designed like a suitcase, to be lugged around and laid on its side to be used. Besides portability, the Compaq was successful because it was fully compatible with the software being run by the IBM PC, which was the standard for business.

In the years that followed, portable computing continued to improve, giving us laptop and notebook computers. The "luggable" computer has given way to a much lighter clamshell computer that weighs from 4 to 6 pounds and runs on batteries. In fact, the most recent advances in technology give us a new class of laptop that is quickly becoming the standard: these laptops are extremely light and portable and use less power than their larger counterparts. The MacBook Air is a good example of this: it weighs less than three pounds and is only 0.68 inches thick!

Finally, as more and more organizations and individuals are moving much of their computing to the Internet, laptops are being developed that use "the cloud" for all of their data and application storage. These laptops are also extremely light because they have no need of a hard disk at all! A good example of this type of laptop (sometimes called a netbook) is Samsung's Chromebook.

Smartphones

The first modern-day mobile phone was invented in 1973. Resembling a brick and weighing in at two pounds, it was priced out of reach for most consumers at nearly four thousand dollars. Since then, mobile phones have become smaller and less expensive; today mobile phones are a modern convenience available to all levels of society. As mobile phones evolved, they became more like small computers. These smartphones have many of the same characteristics as a personal computer, such as an operating system and memory. The first smartphone was the IBM Simon, introduced in 1994.

In January of 2007, Apple introduced the iPhone. Its ease of use and intuitive interface made it an immediate success and solidified the future of smartphones. Running on an operating system called iOS, the iPhone was really a small computer with a touch-screen interface. In 2008, the first Android phone was released, with similar functionality.

Tablet Computers

A tablet computer is one that uses a touch screen as its primary input and is small enough and light enough to be carried around easily. They generally have no keyboard and are self-contained inside a rectangular case. The first tablet computers appeared in the early 2000s and used an attached pen as a writing device for input. These tablets ranged in size from small personal digital assistants (PDAs), which were handheld, to full-sized, 14-inch devices. Most early tablets used a version of an existing computer operating system, such as Windows or Linux.

These early tablet devices were, for the most part, commercial failures. In January, 2010, Apple introduced the iPad, which ushered in a new era of tablet computing. Instead of a pen, the iPad used the finger as the primary input device. Instead of using the operating system of their desktop and laptop computers, Apple chose to use iOS, the operating system of the iPhone. Because the iPad had a user interface that was the same as the iPhone, consumers felt comfortable and sales took off. The iPad has set the standard for tablet computing. After the success of the iPad, computer manufacturers began to develop new tablets that utilized operating systems that were designed for mobile devices, such as Android.

The Rise of Mobile Computing

Mobile computing is having a huge impact on the business world today. The use of smartphones and tablet computers is rising at double-digit rates each year. The Gartner Group, in a report issued in April, 2013, estimates that over 1.7 million mobile phones will ship in the US in 2013 as compared to just over 340,000 personal computers. Over half of these mobile phones are smartphones.[2] Almost 200,000 tablet computers are predicted to ship in 2013. According to the report, PC shipments will continue to decline as phone and tablet shipments continue to increase. [3]

Integrated Computing

Along with advances in computers themselves, computing technology is being integrated into many everyday products. From automobiles to refrigerators to airplanes, computing technology is enhancing what these devices can do and is adding capabilities that would have been considered science fiction just a few years ago. Here are two of the latest ways that computing technologies are being integrated into everyday products:

- The Smart House
- The Self-Driving Car

The Commoditization of the Personal Computer

Over the past thirty years, as the personal computer has gone from technical marvel to part of our everyday lives, it has also become a commodity. The PC has become a commodity in the sense that there is very little differentiation between computers, and the primary factor that controls their sale is their price. Hundreds of manufacturers all over the world now create parts for personal computers. Dozens of companies buy these parts and assemble the computers. As commodities, there are essentially no differences between computers made by these different companies. Profit margins for personal computers are razor-thin, leading hardware developers to find the lowest-cost manufacturing.

There is one brand of computer for which this is not the case – Apple. Because Apple does not make computers that run on the same open standards as other manufacturers, they can make a unique product that no one can easily copy. By creating what many consider to be a superior product, Apple can charge more

2. Smartphone shipments to surpass feature phones this year. CNet, June 4, 2013. http://news.cnet.com/8301-1035_3-57587583-94/
    smartphone-shipments-to-surpass-feature-phones-this-year/
3. Gartner Press Release. April 4, 2013. http://www.gartner.com/newsroom/id/2408515

for their computers than other manufacturers. Just as with the iPad and iPhone, Apple has chosen a strategy of differentiation, which, at least at this time, seems to be paying off.

The Problem of Electronic Waste

Electronic waste (Public Domain)

Personal computers have been around for over thirty-five years. Millions of them have been used and discarded. Mobile phones are now available in even the remotest parts of the world and, after a few years of use, they are discarded. Where does this electronic debris end up?

Often, it gets routed to any country that will accept it. Many times, it ends up in dumps in developing nations. These dumps are beginning to be seen as health hazards for those living near them. Though many manufacturers have made strides in using materials that can be recycled, electronic waste is a problem with which we must all deal.

Summary

Information systems hardware consists of the components of digital technology that you can touch. In this chapter, we reviewed the components that make up a personal computer, with the understanding that the configuration of a personal computer is very similar to that of any type of digital computing device. A personal computer is made up of many components, most importantly the CPU, motherboard, RAM, hard disk, removable media, and input/output devices. We also reviewed some variations on the personal computer, such as the tablet computer and the smartphone. In accordance with Moore's Law, these technologies have improved quickly over the years, making today's computing devices much more powerful than devices just a few years ago. Finally, we discussed two of the consequences of this evolution: the commoditization of the personal computer and the problem of electronic waste.

Study Questions

1. Write your own description of what the term *information systems hardware* means.

2. What is the impact of Moore's Law on the various hardware components described in this chapter?

3. Write a summary of one of the items linked to in the "Integrated Computing" section.

4. Explain why the personal computer is now considered a commodity.

5. The CPU can also be thought of as the _____ of the computer.

6. List the following in increasing order (slowest to fastest): megahertz, kilohertz, gigahertz.

7. What is the bus of a computer?

8. Name two differences between RAM and a hard disk.

9. What are the advantages of solid-state drives over hard disks?

10. How heavy was the first commercially successful portable computer?

Exercises

1. Review the sidebar on the binary number system. How would you represent the number 16 in binary? How about the number 100? Besides decimal and binary, other number bases are used in computing and programming. One of the most used bases is *hexadecimal*, which is base-16. In base-16, the numerals 0 through 9 are supplemented with the letters A (10) through F (15). How would you represent the decimal number 100 in hexadecimal?

2. Review the timeline of computers at the Old Computers website. Pick one computer from the listing and write a brief summary. Include the specifications for CPU, memory, and screen size. Now find the specifications of a computer being offered for sale today and compare. Did Moore's Law hold true?

3. The Homebrew Computer Club was one of the original clubs for enthusiasts of the first personal computer, the Altair 8800. Read some of their newsletters and then discuss some of the issues surrounding this early personal computer.

4. If you could build your own personal computer, what components would you purchase? Put together a list of the components you would use to create it, including a computer case, motherboard, CPU, hard disk, RAM, and DVD drive. How can you be sure they are all compatible with each other? How much would it cost? How does this compare to a similar computer purchased from a vendor such as Dell or HP?

5. Review the Wikipedia entry on electronic waste. Now find at least two more scholarly articles on this topic. Prepare a slideshow that summarizes the issue and then recommend a possible solution based on your research.

6. As with any technology text, there have been advances in technologies since publication. What technology that has been developed recently would you add to this chapter?

7. What is the current state of solid-state drives vs. hard disks? Do original research online where you can compare price on solid-state drives and hard disks. Be sure you note the differences in price, capacity, and speed.

Chapter 3: Software

Learning Objectives

Upon successful completion of this chapter, you will be able to:

- define the term *software*;
- describe the two primary categories of software;
- describe the role ERP software plays in an organization;
- describe cloud computing and its advantages and disadvantages for use in an organization; and
- define the term *open-source* and identify its primary characteristics.

Introduction

The second component of an information system is software. Simply put: Software is the set of instructions that tell the hardware what to do. Software is created through the process of programming (we will cover the creation of software in more detail in chapter 10). Without software, the hardware would not be functional.

Types of Software

Software can be broadly divided into two categories: operating systems and application software. *Operating systems* manage the hardware and create the interface between the hardware and the user. *Application software* is the category of programs that do something useful for the user.

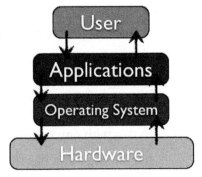

Operating Systems

The operating system provides several essential functions, including:

1. managing the hardware resources of the computer;

2. providing the user-interface components;

3. providing a platform for software developers to write applications.

All computing devices run an operating system. For personal computers, the most popular operating systems are Microsoft's Windows, Apple's OS X, and different versions of Linux. Smartphones and tablets run operating systems as well, such as Apple's iOS, Google's Android, Microsoft's Windows Mobile, and Blackberry.

Early personal-computer operating systems were simple by today's standards; they did not provide multitasking and required the user to type commands to initiate an action. The amount of memory that early operating systems could handle was limited as well, making large programs impractical to run. The most popular of the early operating systems was IBM's Disk Operating System, or DOS, which was actually developed for them by Microsoft.

In 1984, Apple introduced the Macintosh computer, featuring an operating system with a graphical user interface. Though not the first graphical operating system, it was the first one to find commercial success. In 1985, Microsoft released the first version of Windows. This version of Windows was not an operating system, but instead was an application that ran on top of the DOS operating system, providing a graphical environment. It was quite limited and had little commercial success. It was not until the 1990 release of Windows 3.0 that Microsoft found success with a graphical user interface. Because of the hold of IBM and IBM-compatible personal computers on business, it was not until Windows 3.0 was released that business users began using a graphical user interface, ushering us into the graphical-computing era. Since 1990, both Apple and Microsoft have released many new versions of their operating systems, with each release adding the ability to process more data at once and access more memory. Features such as multitasking, virtual memory, and voice input have become standard features of both operating systems.

A third personal-computer operating system family that is gaining in popularity is Linux (pronounced "linn-ex"). Linux is a version of the Unix operating system that runs on the personal computer. Unix is an operating system used primarily by scientists and engineers on larger minicomputers. These are very expensive computers, and software developer Linus Torvalds wanted to find a way to make Unix run on less expensive personal computers. Linux was the result. Linux has many variations and now powers a large percentage of web servers in the world. It is also an example of *open-source software*, a topic we will cover later in this chapter.

Linux logo
(Copyright: Larry Ewing)

Sidebar: Mac vs. Windows

Are you a Mac? Are you a PC? Ever since its introduction in 1984, users of the Apple Macintosh have been quite biased about their preference for the Macintosh operating system (now called OS X) over Microsoft's. When Microsoft introduced Windows, Apple sued Microsoft, claiming that they copied the "look and feel" of the Macintosh operating system. In the end, Microsoft successfully defended themselves.

Over the past few years, Microsoft and Apple have traded barbs with each other, each claiming to have a better operating system and software. While Microsoft has always had the larger market share (see sidebar), Apple has been the favorite of artists, musicians, and the technology elite. Apple also provides a lot of computers to elementary schools, thus gaining a following among the younger generation.

Sidebar: Why Is Microsoft Software So Dominant in the Business World?

If you've worked in the world of business, you may have noticed that almost all of the computers run a version of Microsoft's Windows operating system. Why is this? On almost all college campuses, you see a preponderance of Apple Macintosh laptops. In elementary schools, Apple reigns as well. Why has this not extended into the business world?

As we learned in chapter 1, almost all businesses used IBM mainframe computers back in the 1960s and 1970s. These same businesses shied away from personal computers until IBM released the PC in 1981.

When executives had to make a decision about purchasing personal computers for their employees, they would choose the safe route and purchase IBM. The saying then was: "No one ever got fired for buying IBM." So over the next decade, companies bought IBM personal computers (or those compatible with them), which ran an operating system called DOS. DOS was created by Microsoft, so when Microsoft released Windows as the next iteration of DOS, companies took the safe route and started purchasing Windows.

Microsoft soon found itself with the dominant personal-computer operating system for businesses. As the networked personal computer began to replace the mainframe computer as the primary way of computing inside businesses, it became essential for Microsoft to give businesses the ability to administer and secure their networks. Microsoft developed business-level server products to go along with their personal computer products, thereby providing a complete business solution. And so now, the saying goes: "No one ever got fired for buying Microsoft."

Application Software

The second major category of software is application software. Application software is, essentially, software that allows the user to accomplish some goal or purpose. For example, if you have to write a paper, you might use the application-software program Microsoft Word. If you want to listen to music, you might use iTunes. To surf the web, you might use Internet Explorer or Firefox. Even a computer game could be considered application software.

The "Killer" App

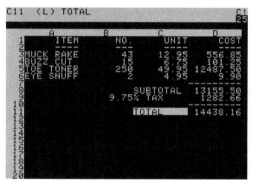

VisiCalc running on an Apple II. (Public Domain)

When a new type of digital device is invented, there are generally a small group of technology enthusiasts who will purchase it just for the joy of figuring out how it works. However, for most of us, until a device can actually do something useful we are not going to spend our hard-earned money on it. A "killer" application is one that becomes so essential that large numbers of people will buy a device just to run that application. For the personal computer, the killer application was the spreadsheet. In 1979, VisiCalc, the first personal-computer spreadsheet package, was introduced. It was an immediate hit and drove sales of the Apple II. It also solidified the value of the personal computer beyond the relatively small circle of technology geeks. When the IBM PC was released, another spreadsheet program, Lotus 1-2-3, was the killer app for business users.

Productivity Software

Along with the spreadsheet, several other software applications have become standard tools for the workplace. These applications, called productivity software, allow office employees to complete their daily work. Many times, these applications come packaged together, such as in Microsoft's Office suite. Here is a list of these applications and their basic functions:

- Word processing: This class of software provides for the creation of written documents. Functions include the ability to type and edit text, format fonts and paragraphs, and add, move, and delete text throughout the document. Most modern word-processing programs also have the ability to add tables, images, and various layout and formatting features to the document. Word processors save their documents as electronic files in a variety of formats. By far, the most popular word-processing package is Microsoft Word, which saves its files in the DOCX format. This format can be read/written by many other word-processor packages.

- Spreadsheet: This class of software provides a way to do numeric calculations and analysis. The working area is divided into rows and columns, where users can enter numbers, text, or formulas. It is the formulas that make a spreadsheet powerful, allowing the user to develop complex calculations that can change based on the numbers entered. Most spreadsheets also include the ability to create charts based on the data entered. The most popular spreadsheet package is Microsoft Excel, which saves its files in the XLSX format. Just as with word processors, many other spreadsheet packages can read and write to this file format.

- Presentation: This class of software provides for the creation of slideshow presentations. Harkening back to the days of overhead projectors and transparencies, presentation software allows its users to create a set of slides that can be printed or projected on a screen. Users can add text, images, and other media elements to the slides. Microsoft's PowerPoint is the most popular software right now, saving its files in PPTX format.

- Some office suites include other types of software. For example, Microsoft Office includes Outlook, its e-mail package, and OneNote, an information-gathering collaboration tool. The professional version of Office also includes Microsoft Access, a database package. (Databases are covered more in chapter 4.)

Microsoft popularized the idea of the office-software productivity bundle with their release of Microsoft Office. This package continues to dominate the market and most businesses expect employees to know how to use this software. However, many competitors to Microsoft Office do exist and are compatible with the file formats used by Microsoft (see table below). Recently, Microsoft has begun to offer a web version of their Office suite. Similar to Google Drive, this suite allows users to edit and share documents online utilizing cloud-computing technology. Cloud computing will be discussed later in this chapter.

Category: Suite:	Word Processing	Spreadsheet	Presentation	Other
Microsoft Office	Word	Excel	PowerPoint	Outlook (email), Access (database), OneNote (information gathering)
Apple iWork	Pages	Numbers	Keynote	Integrates with iTunes, iCloud, and other Apple software
OpenOffice	Writer	Calc	Impress	Base (database), Draw (drawing), Math (equations)
Google Drive	Document	Spreadsheet	Presentation	Gmail (email), Forms (online form data collection), Draw (drawing)

Comparison of office application software suites

Utility Software and Programming Software

Two subcategories of application software worth mentioning are utility software and programming software. Utility software includes software that allows you to fix or modify your computer in some way. Examples include antivirus software and disk defragmentation software. These types of software packages were invented to fill shortcomings in operating systems. Many times, a subsequent release of an operating system will include these utility functions as part of the operating system itself.

Programming software is software whose purpose is to make more software. Most of these programs provide programmers with an environment in which they can write the code, test it, and convert it into the format that can then be run on a computer.

Sidebar: "PowerPointed" to Death

As presentation software, specifically Microsoft PowerPoint, has gained acceptance as the primary method to formally present information in a business setting, the art of giving an engaging presentation is becoming rare. Many presenters now just read the bullet points in the presentation and immediately bore those in attendance, who can already read it for themselves.

The real problem is not with PowerPoint as much as it is with the person creating and presenting. Author and thinker Seth Godin put it this way: "PowerPoint could be the most powerful tool on your computer. But it's not. It's actually a dismal failure. Almost every PowerPoint presentation sucks rotten eggs."[1] The software used to help you communicate should not duplicate the presentation you want to give, but instead

1. From *Why are your PowerPoints so bad?* available for download at http://www.sethgodin.com/freeprize/reallybad-1.pdf.

it should support it. I highly recommend the book *Presentation Zen* by Garr Reynolds to anyone who wants to improve their presentation skills.

Software developers are becoming aware of this problem as well. New digital presentation technologies are being developed, with the hopes of becoming "the next PowerPoint." One innovative new presentation application is Prezi. Prezi is a presentation tool that uses a single canvas for the presentation, allowing presenters to place text, images, and other media on the canvas, and then navigate between these objects as they present. Just as with PowerPoint, Prezi should be used to supplement the presentation. And we must always remember that sometimes the best presentations are made with no digital tools.

Sidebar: I Own This Software, Right? Well . . .

When you purchase software and install it on your computer, are you the owner of that software? Technically, you are not! When you install software, you are actually just being given a license to use it. When you first install a software package, you are asked to agree to the terms of service or the license agreement. In that agreement, you will find that your rights to use the software are limited. For example, in the terms of the Microsoft Office Excel 2010 software license, you will find the following statement: "This software is licensed, not sold. This agreement only gives you some rights to use the features included in the software edition you licensed."

For the most part, these restrictions are what you would expect: you cannot make illegal copies of the software and you may not use it to do anything illegal. However, there are other, more unexpected terms in these software agreements. For example, many software agreements ask you to agree to a limit on liability. Again, from Microsoft: "Limitation on and exclusion of damages. You can recover from Microsoft and its suppliers only direct damages up to the amount you paid for the software. You cannot recover any other damages, including consequential, lost profits, special, indirect or incidental damages." What this means is that if a problem with the software causes harm to your business, you cannot hold Microsoft or the supplier responsible for damages.

Applications for the Enterprise

As the personal computer proliferated inside organizations, control over the information generated by the organization began splintering. Say the customer service department creates a customer database to keep track of calls and problem reports, and the sales department also creates a database to keep track of customer information. Which one should be used as the master list of customers? As another example, someone in sales might create a spreadsheet to calculate sales revenue, while someone in finance creates a different one that meets the needs of their department. However, it is likely that the two spreadsheets will come up with different totals for revenue. Which one is correct? And who is managing all of this information?

Enterprise Resource Planning

In the 1990s, the need to bring the organization's information back under centralized control became more apparent. The enterprise resource planning (ERP) system (sometimes just called enterprise software) was developed to bring together an entire organization in one software application. Simply put, an ERP system is a software application utilizing a central database that is implemented throughout the entire organization. Let's take a closer look at this definition:

- "A software application": An ERP is a software application that is used by many of an organization's employees.
- "utilizing a central database": All users of the ERP edit and save their information from the data source. What this means practically is that there is only one customer database, there is only one calculation for revenue, etc.
- "that is implemented throughout the entire organization": ERP systems include functionality that covers all of the essential components of a business. Further, an organization can purchase modules for its ERP system that match specific needs, such as manufacturing or planning.

Registered trademark of SAP

ERP systems were originally marketed to large corporations. However, as more and more large companies began installing them, ERP vendors began targeting mid-sized and even smaller businesses. Some of the more well-known ERP systems include those from SAP, Oracle, and Microsoft.

In order to effectively implement an ERP system in an organization, the organization must be ready to make a full commitment. All aspects of the organization are affected as old systems are replaced by the ERP system. In general, implementing an ERP system can take two to three years and several million dollars. In most cases, the cost of the software is not the most expensive part of the implementation: it is the cost of the consultants!

So why implement an ERP system? If done properly, an ERP system can bring an organization a good return on their investment. By consolidating information systems across the enterprise and using the software to enforce best practices, most organizations see an overall improvement after implementing an ERP. Business processes as a form of competitive advantage will be covered in chapter 9.

Sidebar: Y2K and ERP

The initial wave of software-application development began in the 1960s, when applications were developed for mainframe computers. In those days, computing was expensive, so applications were designed to take as little space as possible. One shortcut that many programmers took was in the storage of dates, specifically the year. Instead of allocating four digits to hold the year, many programs allocated two digits, making the assumption that the first two digits were "19″. For example, to calculate how old someone was, the application would take the last two digits of the current year (for 1995, for example, that would be "95″) and then subtract the two digits stored for the birthday year ("65″ for 1965). 95 minus 65 gives an age of 30, which is correct.

However, as the year 2000 approached, many of these "legacy" applications were still being used, and businesses were very concerned that any software applications they were using that needed to calculate dates would fail. To update our age-calculation example, the application would take the last two digits of the current year (for 2012, that would be "12″) and then subtract the two digits stored for the birthday year ("65″ for 1965). 12 minus 65 gives an age of -53, which would cause an error. In order to solve this problem, applications would have to be updated to use four digits for years instead of two. Solving this would be a massive undertaking, as every line of code and every database would have to be examined.

This is where companies gained additional incentive to implement an ERP system. For many organizations that were considering upgrading to ERP systems in the late 1990s, this problem, known as Y2K (year 2000), gave them the extra push they needed to get their ERP installed before the year 2000. ERP vendors guaranteed that their systems had been designed to be Y2K compliant – which simply meant that they stored dates using four digits instead of two. This led to a massive increase in ERP installations in the years leading up to 2000, making the ERP a standard software application for businesses.

Customer Relationship Management

A customer relationship management (CRM) system is a software application designed to manage an organization's customers. In today's environment, it is important to develop relationships with your customers, and the use of a well-designed CRM can allow a business to personalize its relationship with each of its customers. Some ERP software systems include CRM modules. An example of a well-known CRM package is Salesforce.

Supply Chain Management

Many organizations must deal with the complex task of managing their supply chains. At its simplest, a supply chain is the linkage between an organization's suppliers, its manufacturing facilities, and the distributors of its products. Each link in the chain has a multiplying effect on the complexity of the process: if there are two suppliers, one manufacturing facility, and two distributors, for example, then there are 2 x 1 x 2 = 4 links to handle. However, if you add two more suppliers, another manufacturing facility, and two more distributors, then you have 4 x 2 x 4 = 32 links to manage.

A supply chain management (SCM) system manages the interconnection between these links, as well as the inventory of the products in their various stages of development. A full definition of a supply chain management system is provided by the Association for Operations Management: "The design, planning, execution, control, and monitoring of supply chain activities with the objective of creating net value, building a competitive infrastructure, leveraging worldwide logistics, synchronizing supply with demand, and measuring performance globally."[2] Most ERP systems include a supply chain management module.

Mobile Applications

Just as with the personal computer, mobile devices such as tablet computers and smartphones also have operating systems and application software. In fact, these mobile devices are in many ways just smaller versions of personal computers. A mobile app is a software application programmed to run specifically on a mobile device.

---

2. http://www.apics.org/dictionary/dictionary-information?ID=3984

As we saw in chapter 2, smartphones and tablets are becoming a dominant form of computing, with many more smartphones being sold than personal computers. This means that organizations will have to get smart about developing software on mobile devices in order to stay relevant.

These days, most mobile devices run on one of two operating systems: Android or iOS. Android is an open-source operating system purchased and supported by Google; iOS is Apple's mobile operating system. In the fourth quarter of 2012, Android was installed on 70.1% of all mobile phones shipped, followed by 21.0% for iOS. Other mobile operating systems of note are Blackberry (3.2%) and Windows (2.6%). [3]

As organizations consider making their digital presence compatible with mobile devices, they will have to decide whether to build a mobile app. A mobile app is an expensive proposition, and it will only run on one type of mobile device at a time. For example, if an organization creates an iPhone app, those with Android phones cannot run the application. Each app takes several thousand dollars to create, so this is not a trivial decision for many companies.

One option many companies have is to create a website that is mobile-friendly. A mobile website works on all mobile devices and costs about the same as creating an app. We will discuss the question of whether to build a mobile app more thoroughly in Chapter 10.

Cloud Computing

Historically, for software to run on a computer, an individual copy of the software had to be installed on the computer, either from a disk or, more recently, after being downloaded from the Internet. The concept of "cloud" computing changes this, however.

To understand cloud computing, we first have to understand what the cloud is. "The cloud" refers to applications, services, and data storage on the Internet. These service providers rely on giant server farms and massive storage devices that are connected via Internet protocols. Cloud computing is the use of these services by individuals and organizations.

You probably already use cloud computing in some forms. For example, if you access your e-mail via your web browser, you are using a form of cloud computing. If you use Google Drive's applications, you are using cloud computing. While these are free versions of cloud computing, there is big business in providing applications and data storage over the web. Salesforce (see above) is a good example of cloud computing – their entire suite of CRM applications are offered via the cloud. Cloud computing is not limited to web applications: it can also be used for services such as phone or video streaming.

Advantages of Cloud Computing

- No software to install or upgrades to maintain.
- Available from any computer that has access to the Internet.
- Can scale to a large number of users easily.
- New applications can be up and running very quickly.
- Services can be leased for a limited time on an as-needed basis.
- Your information is not lost if your hard disk crashes or your laptop is stolen.
- You are not limited by the available memory or disk space on your computer.

3. Taken from IDC Worldwide Mobile Phone Tracker, February 14, 2013. Full report available at http://www.idc.com/getdoc.jsp?containerId=prUS23946013

Disadvantages of Cloud Computing

- Your information is stored on someone else's computer – how safe is it?
- You must have Internet access to use it. If you do not have access, you're out of luck.
- You are relying on a third-party to provide these services.

Cloud computing has the ability to really impact how organizations manage technology. For example, why is an IT department needed to purchase, configure, and manage personal computers and software when all that is really needed is an Internet connection?

Using a Private Cloud

Many organizations are understandably nervous about giving up control of their data and some of their applications by using cloud computing. But they also see the value in reducing the need for installing software and adding disk storage to local computers. A solution to this problem lies in the concept of a *private cloud*. While there are various models of a private cloud, the basic idea is for the cloud service provider to section off web server space for a specific organization. The organization has full control over that server space while still gaining some of the benefits of cloud computing.

Virtualization

One technology that is utilized extensively as part of cloud computing is "virtualization." Virtualization is the process of using software to simulate a computer or some other device. For example, using virtualization, a single computer can perform the functions of several computers. Companies such as EMC provide virtualization software that allows cloud service providers to provision web servers to their clients quickly and efficiently. Organizations are also implementing virtualization in order to reduce the number of servers needed to provide the necessary services. For more detail on how virtualization works, see this informational page from VMWare.

Software Creation

How is software created? If software is the set of instructions that tells the hardware what to do, how are these instructions written? If a computer reads everything as ones and zeroes, do we have to learn how to write software that way?

Modern software applications are written using a programming language. A programming language consists of a set of commands and syntax that can be organized logically to execute specific functions. This language generally consists of a set of readable words combined with symbols. Using this language, a programmer writes a program (called the source code) that can then be compiled into machine-readable form, the ones and zeroes necessary to be executed by the CPU. Examples of well-known programming languages today include Java, PHP, and various flavors of C (Visual C, C++, C#). Languages such as HTML and Javascript are used to develop web pages. Most of the time, programming is done inside a programming environment; when you purchase a copy of Visual Studio from Microsoft, it provides you with an editor, compiler, and help for many of Microsoft's programming languages.

Software programming was originally an individual process, with each programmer working on an entire program, or several programmers each working on a portion of a larger program. However, newer methods of software development include a more collaborative approach, with teams of programmers working on code together. We will cover information-systems development more fully in chapter 10.

Open-Source Software

When the personal computer was first released, it did not serve any practical need. Early computers were difficult to program and required great attention to detail. However, many personal-computer enthusiasts immediately banded together to build applications and solve problems. These computer enthusiasts were happy to share any programs they built and solutions to problems they found; this collaboration enabled them to more quickly innovate and fix problems.

As software began to become a business, however, this idea of sharing everything fell out of favor, at least with some. When a software program takes hundreds of man-hours to develop, it is understandable that the programmers do not want to just give it away. This led to a new business model of restrictive software licensing, which required payment for software, a model that is still dominant today. This model is sometimes referred to as *closed source*, as the source code is not made available to others.

There are many, however, who feel that software should not be restricted. Just as with those early hobbyists in the 1970s, they feel that innovation and progress can be made much more rapidly if we share what we learn. In the 1990s, with Internet access connecting more and more people together, the open-source movement gained steam.

Open-source software is software that makes the source code available for anyone to copy and use. For most of us, having access to the source code of a program does us little good, as we are not programmers and won't be able to do much with it. The good news is that open-source software is also available in a compiled format that we can simply download and install. The open-source movement has led to the development of some of the most-used software in the world, including the Firefox browser, the Linux operating system, and the Apache web server. Many also think open-source software is superior to closed-source software. Because the source code is freely available, many programmers have contributed to open-source software projects, adding features and fixing bugs.

Many businesses are wary of open-source software precisely because the code is available for anyone to see. They feel that this increases the risk of an attack. Others counter that this openness actually decreases the risk because the code is exposed to thousands of programmers who can incorporate code changes to quickly patch vulnerabilities.

There are many arguments on both sides of the aisle for the benefits of the two models. Some benefits of the open-source model are:

- The software is available for free.
- The software source-code is available; it can be examined and reviewed before it is installed.
- The large community of programmers who work on open-source projects leads to quick bug-fixing and feature additions.

Some benefits of the closed-source model are:

- By providing financial incentive for software development, some of the brightest minds have chosen software development as a career.
- Technical support from the company that developed the software.

Today there are thousands of open-source software applications available for download. For example, as we discussed previously in this chapter, you can get the productivity suite from Open Office. One good place to search for open-source software is sourceforge.net, where thousands of software applications are available for free download.

Summary

Software gives the instructions that tell the hardware what to do. There are two basic categories of software: operating systems and applications. Operating systems provide access to the computer hardware and make system resources available. Application software is designed to meet a specific goal. Productivity software is a subset of application software that provides basic business functionality to a personal computer: word processing, spreadsheets, and presentations. An ERP system is a software application with a centralized database that is implemented across the entire organization. Cloud computing is a method of software delivery that runs on any computer that has a web browser and access to the Internet. Software is developed through a process called programming, in which a programmer uses a programming language to put together the logic needed to create the program. While most software is developed using a closed-source model, the open-source movement is gaining more support today.

Study Questions

1. Come up with your own definition of software. Explain the key terms in your definition.

2. What are the functions of the operating system?

3. Which of the following are operating systems and which are applications: Microsoft Excel, Google Chrome, iTunes, Windows, Android, Angry Birds.

4. What is your favorite software application? What tasks does it help you accomplish?

5. What is a "killer" app? What was the killer app for the PC?

6. How would you categorize the software that runs on mobile devices? Break down these apps into at least three basic categories and give an example of each.

7. Explain what an ERP system does.

8. What is open-source software? How does it differ from closed-source software? Give an example of each.

9. What does a software license grant?

10. How did the Y2K (year 2000) problem affect the sales of ERP systems?

Exercises

1. Go online and find a case study about the implementation of an ERP system. Was it successful? How long did it take? Does the case study tell you how much money the organization spent?

2. What ERP system does your university or place of employment use? Find out which one they use and see how it compares to other ERP systems.

3. If you were running a small business with limited funds for information technology, would you consider using cloud computing? Find some web-based resources that support your decision.

4. Download and install Open Office. Use it to create a document or spreadsheet. How does it compare to Microsoft Office? Does the fact that you got it for free make it feel less valuable?

5. Go to sourceforge.net and review their most downloaded software applications. Report back on the variety of applications you find. Then pick one that interests you and report back on what it does, the kind of technical support offered, and the user reviews.

6. Review this article on the security risks of open-source software. Write a short analysis giving your opinion on the different risks discussed.

7. What are three examples of programming languages? What makes each of these languages useful to programmers?

Chapter 4: Data and Databases

Learning Objectives

Upon successful completion of this chapter, you will be able to:

- describe the differences between data, information, and knowledge;
- define the term *database* and identify the steps to creating one;
- describe the role of a database management system;
- describe the characteristics of a data warehouse; and
- define data mining and describe its role in an organization.

Introduction

You have already been introduced to the first two components of information systems: hardware and software. However, those two components by themselves do not make a computer useful. Imagine if you turned on a computer, started the word processor, but could not save a document. Imagine if you opened a music player but there was no music to play. Imagine opening a web browser but there were no web pages. Without data, hardware and software are not very useful! Data is the third component of an information system.

Data, Information, and Knowledge

Data are the raw bits and pieces of information with no context. If I told you, "15, 23, 14, 85," you would not have learned anything. But I would have given you data.

Data can be quantitative or qualitative. Quantitative data is numeric, the result of a measurement, count, or some other mathematical calculation. Qualitative data is descriptive. "Ruby Red," the color of a 2013 Ford Focus, is an example of qualitative data. A number can be qualitative too: if I tell you my favorite number is 5, that is qualitative data because it is descriptive, not the result of a measurement or mathematical calculation.

By itself, data is not that useful. To be useful, it needs to be given context. Returning to the example above, if I told you that "15, 23, 14, and 85" are the numbers of students that had registered for upcoming classes, that would be *information*. By adding the context – that the numbers represent the count of students registering for specific classes – I have converted data into information.

Once we have put our data into context, aggregated and analyzed it, we can use it to make decisions for our organization. We can say that this consumption of information produces *knowledge*. This knowledge can be used to make decisions, set policies, and even spark innovation.

The final step up the information ladder is the step from knowledge (knowing a lot about a topic) to *wisdom*. We can say that someone has wisdom when they can combine their knowledge and experience to produce a deeper understanding of a topic. It often takes many years to develop wisdom on a particular topic, and requires patience.

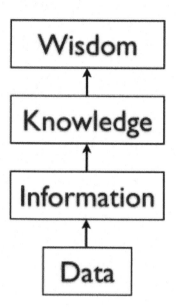

Examples of Data

Almost all software programs require data to do anything useful. For example, if you are editing a document in a word processor such as Microsoft Word, the document you are working on is the data. The word-processing software can manipulate the data: create a new document, duplicate a document, or modify a document. Some other examples of data are: an MP3 music file, a video file, a spreadsheet, a web page, and an e-book. In some cases, such as with an e-book, you may only have the ability to read the data.

Databases

The goal of many information systems is to transform data into information in order to generate knowledge that can be used for decision making. In order to do this, the system must be able to take data, put the data into context, and provide tools for aggregation and analysis. A database is designed for just such a purpose.

A database is an organized collection of related information. It is an *organized* collection, because in a database, all data is described and associated with other data. All information in a database should be *related* as well; separate databases should be created to manage unrelated information. For example, a database that contains information about students should not also hold information about company stock prices. Databases are not always digital – a filing cabinet, for instance, might be considered a form of database. For the purposes of this text, we will only consider digital databases.

Relational Databases

Databases can be organized in many different ways, and thus take many forms. The most popular form of database today is the relational database. Popular examples of relational databases are Microsoft Access, MySQL, and Oracle. A relational database is one in which data is organized into one or more tables. Each table has a set of fields, which define the nature of the data stored in the table. A record is one instance of a set of fields in a table. To visualize this, think of the records as the rows of the table and the fields as the columns of the table. In the example below, we have a table of student information, with each row representing a student and each column representing one piece of information about the student.

Fields (Columns)

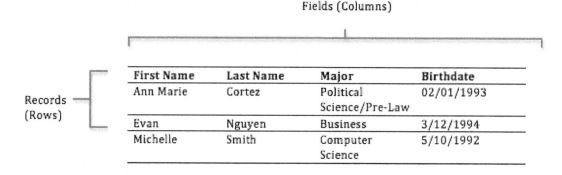

	First Name	Last Name	Major	Birthdate
Records (Rows)	Ann Marie	Cortez	Political Science/Pre-Law	02/01/1993
	Evan	Nguyen	Business	3/12/1994
	Michelle	Smith	Computer Science	5/10/1992

Rows and columns in a table

In a relational database, all the tables are related by one or more fields, so that it is possible to connect all the tables in the database through the field(s) they have in common. For each table, one of the fields is identified as a primary key. This key is the unique identifier for each record in the table. To help you understand these terms further, let's walk through the process of designing a database.

Designing a Database

Suppose a university wants to create an information system to track participation in student clubs. After interviewing several people, the design team learns that the goal of implementing the system is to give better insight into how the university funds clubs. This will be accomplished by tracking how many members each club has and how active the clubs are. From this, the team decides that the system must keep track of the clubs, their members, and their events. Using this information, the design team determines that the following tables need to be created:

- Clubs: this will track the club name, the club president, and a short description of the club.
- Students: student name, e-mail, and year of birth.
- Memberships: this table will correlate students with clubs, allowing us to have any given student join multiple clubs.
- Events: this table will track when the clubs meet and how many students showed up.

Now that the design team has determined which tables to create, they need to define the specific information that each table will hold. This requires identifying the fields that will be in each table. For example, Club Name would be one of the fields in the Clubs table. First Name and Last Name would be fields in the Students table. Finally, since this will be a relational database, every table should have a field in common with at least one other table (in other words: they should have a relationship with each other).

In order to properly create this relationship, a primary key must be selected for each table. This key is a unique identifier for each record in the table. For example, in the Students table, it might be possible to use students' last name as a way to uniquely identify them. However, it is more than likely that some students will share a last name (like Rodriguez, Smith, or Lee), so a different field should be selected. A student's e-mail address might be a good choice for a primary key, since e-mail addresses are unique. However, a primary key cannot change, so this would mean that if students changed their e-mail address we would have to remove them from the database and then re-insert them – not an attractive proposition. Our solution is to create a value for each student — a user ID — that will act as a primary key. We will also do this for each of the student clubs. This solution is quite common and is the reason you have so many user IDs!

You can see the final database design in the figure below:

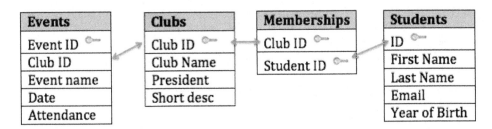

Student Clubs database diagram

With this design, not only do we have a way to organize all of the information we need to meet the requirements, but we have also successfully related all the tables together. Here's what the database tables might look like with some sample data. Note that the Memberships table has the sole purpose of allowing us to relate multiple students to multiple clubs.

Club ID	Club name	President	Short desc
1	Cheese Club	14	To talk about our love of cheese.
2	Chess Club	1	To learn how to become better chess players.
3	Archery Club	6	To compete in archery tournaments.

Table: Clubs

ID	First Name	Last Name	Email	Year of Birth
1	Peter	Lee	plee@university.edu	1992
2	Jonathan	Edwards	jedwards@university.edu	1994
3	Marilyn	Johnson	mjohnson@university.edu	1993
6	Joe	Kim	jkim@university.edu	1992
12	Haley	Martinez	hmartinez@university.edu	1993
14	John	Mfume	jmfume@university.edu	1991
15	David	Letty	dletty@university.edu	1995

Table: Students

Club ID	Student ID
1	1
1	2
1	14
2	1
2	3
2	5
2	6
3	1
3	6
3	12
3	14
3	15

Table: Memberships

Club ID	Event name	Date	Attendance
1	Cheese promo	1/10/2013	6
2	MLK Tournament	1/21/2013	17
3	January meeting	1/22/2013	12
2	January meeting	1/28/2013	10

Table: Events

Normalization

When designing a database, one important concept to understand is *normalization*. In simple terms, to normalize a database means to design it in a way that: 1) reduces duplication of data between tables and 2) gives the table as much flexibility as possible.

In the Student Clubs database design, the design team worked to achieve these objectives. For example, to track memberships, a simple solution might have been to create a Members field in the Clubs table and then just list the names of all of the members there. However, this design would mean that if a student joined two clubs, then his or her information would have to be entered a second time. Instead, the designers solved this problem by using two tables: Students and Memberships.

In this design, when a student joins their first club, we first must add the student to the Students table, where their first name, last name, e-mail address, and birth year are entered. This addition to the Students table will generate a student ID. Now we will add a new entry to denote that the student is a member of a specific club. This is accomplished by adding a record with the student ID and the club ID in the Memberships table. If this student joins a second club, we do not have to duplicate the entry of the student's name, e-mail, and birth year; instead, we only need to make another entry in the Memberships table of the second club's ID and the student's ID.

The design of the Student Clubs database also makes it simple to change the design without major modifications to the existing structure. For example, if the design team were asked to add functionality to the system to track faculty advisors to the clubs, we could easily accomplish this by adding a Faculty Advisors table (similar to the Students table) and then adding a new field to the Clubs table to hold the Faculty Advisor ID.

Data Types

When defining the fields in a database table, we must give each field a data type. For example, the field Birth Year is a year, so it will be a number, while First Name will be text. Most modern databases allow for several different data types to be stored. Some of the more common data types are listed here:

- Text: for storing non-numeric data that is brief, generally under 256 characters. The database designer can identify the maximum length of the text.
- Number: for storing numbers. There are usually a few different number types that can be selected, depending on how large the largest number will be.
- Yes/No: a special form of the number data type that is (usually) one byte long, with a 0 for "No" or "False" and a 1 for "Yes" or "True".
- Date/Time: a special form of the number data type that can be interpreted as a number or a time.
- Currency: a special form of the number data type that formats all values with a currency indicator and two decimal places.

- Paragraph Text: this data type allows for text longer than 256 characters.
- Object: this data type allows for the storage of data that cannot be entered via keyboard, such as an image or a music file.

There are two important reasons that we must properly define the data type of a field. First, a data type tells the database what functions can be performed with the data. For example, if we wish to perform mathematical functions with one of the fields, we must be sure to tell the database that the field is a number data type. So if we have, say, a field storing birth year, we can subtract the number stored in that field from the current year to get age.

The second important reason to define data type is so that the proper amount of storage space is allocated for our data. For example, if the First Name field is defined as a text(50) data type, this means fifty characters are allocated for each first name we want to store. However, even if the first name is only five characters long, fifty characters (bytes) will be allocated. While this may not seem like a big deal, if our table ends up holding 50,000 names, we are allocating 50 * 50,000 = 2,500,000 bytes for storage of these values. It may be prudent to reduce the size of the field so we do not waste storage space.

Sidebar: The Difference between a Database and a Spreadsheet

Many times, when introducing the concept of databases to students, they quickly decide that a database is pretty much the same as a spreadsheet. After all, a spreadsheet stores data in an organized fashion, using rows and columns, and looks very similar to a database table. This misunderstanding extends beyond the classroom: spreadsheets are used as a substitute for databases in all types of situations every day, all over the world.

To be fair, for simple uses, a spreadsheet can substitute for a database quite well. If a simple listing of rows and columns (a single table) is all that is needed, then creating a database is probably overkill. In our Student Clubs example, if we only needed to track a listing of clubs, the number of members, and the contact information for the president, we could get away with a single spreadsheet. However, the need to include a listing of events and the names of members would be problematic if tracked with a spreadsheet.

When several types of data must be mixed together, or when the relationships between these types of data are complex, then a spreadsheet is not the best solution. A database allows data from several entities (such as students, clubs, memberships, and events) to all be related together into one whole. While a spreadsheet does allow you to define what kinds of values can be entered into its cells, a database provides more intuitive and powerful ways to define the types of data that go into each field, reducing possible errors and allowing for easier analysis.

Though not good for replacing databases, spreadsheets can be ideal tools for analyzing the data stored in a database. A spreadsheet package can be connected to a specific table or query in a database and used to create charts or perform analysis on that data.

Structured Query Language

Once you have a database designed and loaded with data, how will you do something useful with it? The primary way to work with a relational database is to use Structured Query Language, SQL (pronounced "sequel," or simply stated as S-Q-L). Almost all applications that work with databases (such as database management systems, discussed below) make use of SQL as a way to analyze and manipulate relational data. As its name implies, SQL is a language that can be used to work with a relational database. From a simple request for data to a complex update operation, SQL is a mainstay of programmers and database administrators. To give you a taste of what SQL might look like, here are a couple of examples using our Student Clubs database.

- The following query will retrieve a list of the first and last names of the club presidents:

```
SELECT "First Name", "Last Name" FROM "Students" WHERE "Students.ID"
```

- The following query will create a list of the number of students in each club, listing the club name and then the number of members:

```
SELECT "Clubs.Club Name", COUNT("Memberships.Student ID") FROM "Clubs
```

An in-depth description of how SQL works is beyond the scope of this introductory text, but these examples should give you an idea of the power of using SQL to manipulate relational data. Many database packages, such as Microsoft Access, allow you to visually create the query you want to construct and then generate the SQL query for you.

Other Types of Databases

The relational database model is the most used database model today. However, many other database models exist that provide different strengths than the relational model. The hierarchical database model, popular in the 1960s and 1970s, connected data together in a hierarchy, allowing for a parent/child relationship between data. The document-centric model allowed for a more unstructured data storage by placing data into "documents" that could then be manipulated.

Perhaps the most interesting new development is the concept of NoSQL (from the phrase "not only SQL"). NoSQL arose from the need to solve the problem of large-scale databases spread over several servers or even across the world. For a relational database to work properly, it is important that only one person be able to manipulate a piece of data at a time, a concept known as record-locking. But with today's large-scale databases (think Google and Amazon), this is just not possible. A NoSQL database can work with data in a looser way, allowing for a more unstructured environment, communicating changes to the data over time to all the servers that are part of the database.

Database Management Systems

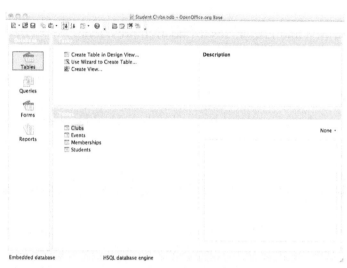

Screen shot of the Open Office database management system

To the computer, a database looks like one or more files. In order for the data in the database to be read, changed, added, or removed, a software program must access it. Many software applications have this ability: iTunes can read its database to give you a listing of its songs (and play the songs); your mobile-phone software can interact with your list of contacts. But what about applications to create or manage a database? What software can you use to create a database, change a database's structure, or simply do analysis? That is the purpose of a category of software applications called database management systems (DBMS).

DBMS packages generally provide an interface to view and change the design of the database, create queries, and develop reports. Most of these packages are designed to work with a specific type of database, but generally are compatible with a wide range of databases.

For example, Apache OpenOffice.org Base (see screen shot) can be used to create, modify, and analyze databases in open-database (ODB) format. Microsoft's Access DBMS is used to work with databases in its own Microsoft Access Database format. Both Access and Base have the ability to read and write to other database formats as well.

Microsoft Access and Open Office Base are examples of personal database-management systems. These systems are primarily used to develop and analyze single-user databases. These databases are not meant to be shared across a network or the Internet, but are instead installed on a particular device and work with a single user at a time.

Enterprise Databases

A database that can only be used by a single user at a time is not going to meet the needs of most organizations. As computers have become networked and are now joined worldwide via the Internet, a class of database has emerged that can be accessed by two, ten, or even a million people. These databases are sometimes installed on a single computer to be accessed by a group of people at a single location. Other times, they are installed over several servers worldwide, meant to be accessed by millions. These relational enterprise database packages are built and supported by companies such as Oracle, Microsoft, and IBM. The open-source MySQL is also an enterprise database.

As stated earlier, the relational database model does not scale well. The term *scale* here refers to a database getting larger and larger, being distributed on a larger number of computers connected via a network. Some companies are looking to provide large-scale database solutions by moving away from the relational model to other, more flexible models. For example, Google now offers the App Engine Datastore, which is based on NoSQL. Developers can use the App Engine Datastore to develop applications that access data from anywhere in the world. Amazon.com offers several database services for enterprise use, including Amazon RDS, which is a relational database service, and Amazon DynamoDB, a NoSQL enterprise solution.

Big Data

A new buzzword that has been capturing the attention of businesses lately is *big data*. The term refers to such massively large data sets that conventional database tools do not have the processing power to analyze them. For example, Walmart must process over one million customer transactions every hour. Storing and analyzing that much data is beyond the power of traditional database-management tools. Understanding the best tools and techniques to manage and analyze these large data sets is a problem that governments and businesses alike are trying to solve.

Sidebar: What Is Metadata?

The term *metadata* can be understood as "data about data." For example, when looking at one of the values of Year of Birth in the Students table, the data itself may be "1992". The metadata about that value would be the field name Year of Birth, the time it was last updated, and the data type (integer). Another example of metadata could be for an MP3 music file, like the one shown in the image below; information such as the length of the song, the artist, the album, the file size, and even the album cover art, are classified as metadata. When a database is being designed, a "data dictionary" is created to hold the metadata, defining the fields and structure of the database.

Data Warehouse

As organizations have begun to utilize databases as the centerpiece of their operations, the need to fully understand and leverage the data they are collecting has become more and more apparent. However, directly analyzing the data that is needed for day-to-day operations is not a good idea; we do not want to tax the operations of the company more than we need to. Further, organizations also want to analyze data in a historical sense: How does the data we have today compare with the same set of data this time last month, or last year? From these needs arose the concept of the data warehouse.

The concept of the data warehouse is simple: extract data from one or more of the organization's databases and load it into the data warehouse (which is itself another database) for storage and analysis. However, the execution of this concept is not that simple. A data warehouse should be designed so that it meets the following criteria:

- It uses non-operational data. This means that the data warehouse is using a copy of data from the active databases that the company uses in its day-to-day operations, so the data warehouse must pull data from the existing databases on a regular, scheduled basis.
- The data is time-variant. This means that whenever data is loaded into the data warehouse, it receives a time stamp, which allows for comparisons between different time periods.
- The data is standardized. Because the data in a data warehouse usually comes from several different sources, it is possible that the data does not use the same definitions or units. For example, our Events table in our Student Clubs database lists the event dates using the mm/dd/

yyyy format (e.g., 01/10/2013). A table in another database might use the format yy/mm/dd (e.g., 13/01/10) for dates. In order for the data warehouse to match up dates, a standard date format would have to be agreed upon and all data loaded into the data warehouse would have to be converted to use this standard format. This process is called extraction-transformation-load (ETL).

There are two primary schools of thought when designing a data warehouse: bottom-up and top-down. The bottom-up approach starts by creating small data warehouses, called data marts, to solve specific business problems. As these data marts are created, they can be combined into a larger data warehouse. The top-down approach suggests that we should start by creating an enterprise-wide data warehouse and then, as specific business needs are identified, create smaller data marts from the data warehouse.

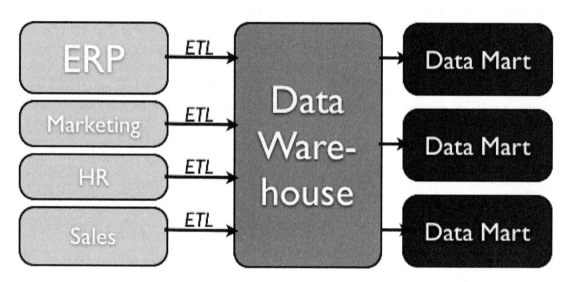

Data warehouse process (top-down)

Benefits of Data Warehouses

Organizations find data warehouses quite beneficial for a number of reasons:

- The process of developing a data warehouse forces an organization to better understand the data that it is currently collecting and, equally important, what data is not being collected.
- A data warehouse provides a centralized view of all data being collected across the enterprise and provides a means for determining data that is inconsistent.
- Once all data is identified as consistent, an organization can generate one version of the truth. This is important when the company wants to report consistent statistics about itself, such as revenue or number of employees.
- By having a data warehouse, snapshots of data can be taken over time. This creates a historical record of data, which allows for an analysis of trends.

- A data warehouse provides tools to combine data, which can provide new information and analysis.

Data Mining

Data mining is the process of analyzing data to find previously unknown trends, patterns, and associations in order to make decisions. Generally, data mining is accomplished through automated means against extremely large data sets, such as a data warehouse. Some examples of data mining include:

- An analysis of sales from a large grocery chain might determine that milk is purchased more frequently the day after it rains in cities with a population of less than 50,000.
- A bank may find that loan applicants whose bank accounts show particular deposit and withdrawal patterns are not good credit risks.
- A baseball team may find that collegiate baseball players with specific statistics in hitting, pitching, and fielding make for more successful major league players.

In some cases, a data-mining project is begun with a hypothetical result in mind. For example, a grocery chain may already have some idea that buying patterns change after it rains and want to get a deeper understanding of exactly what is happening. In other cases, there are no presuppositions and a data-mining program is run against large data sets in order to find patterns and associations.

Privacy Concerns

The increasing power of data mining has caused concerns for many, especially in the area of privacy. In today's digital world, it is becoming easier than ever to take data from disparate sources and combine them to do new forms of analysis. In fact, a whole industry has sprung up around this technology: data brokers. These firms combine publicly accessible data with information obtained from the government and other sources to create vast warehouses of data about people and companies that they can then sell. This subject will be covered in much more detail in chapter 12 – the chapter on the ethical concerns of information systems.

Business Intelligence and Business Analytics

With tools such as data warehousing and data mining at their disposal, businesses are learning how to use information to their advantage. The term *business intelligence* is used to describe the process that organizations use to take data they are collecting and analyze it in the hopes of obtaining a competitive advantage. Besides using data from their internal databases, firms often purchase information from data brokers to get a big-picture understanding of their industries. *Business analytics* is the term used to describe the use of internal company data to improve business processes and practices.

Knowledge Management

We end the chapter with a discussion on the concept of knowledge management (KM). All companies accumulate knowledge over the course of their existence. Some of this knowledge is written down or saved, but not in an organized fashion. Much of this knowledge is not written down; instead, it is stored inside the heads of its employees. Knowledge management is the process of formalizing the capture, indexing, and storing of the company's knowledge in order to benefit from the experiences and insights that the company has captured during its existence.

Summary

In this chapter, we learned about the role that data and databases play in the context of information systems. Data is made up of small facts and information without context. If you give data context, then you have information. Knowledge is gained when information is consumed and used for decision making. A database is an organized collection of related information. Relational databases are the most widely used type of database, where data is structured into tables and all tables must be related to each other through unique identifiers. A database management system (DBMS) is a software application that is used to create and manage databases, and can take the form of a personal DBMS, used by one person, or an enterprise DBMS that can be used by multiple users. A data warehouse is a special form of database that takes data from other databases in an enterprise and organizes it for analysis. Data mining is the process of looking for patterns and relationships in large data sets. Many businesses use databases, data warehouses, and data-mining techniques in order to produce business intelligence and gain a competitive advantage.

Study Questions

1. What is the difference between data, information, and knowledge?

2. Explain in your own words how the data component relates to the hardware and software components of information systems.

3. What is the difference between quantitative data and qualitative data? In what situations could the number 42 be considered qualitative data?

4. What are the characteristics of a relational database?

5. When would using a personal DBMS make sense?

6. What is the difference between a spreadsheet and a database? List three differences between them.

7. Describe what the term *normalization* means.

8. Why is it important to define the data type of a field when designing a relational database?

9. Name a database you interact with frequently. What would some of the field names be?

10. What is metadata?

11. Name three advantages of using a data warehouse.

12. What is data mining?

Exercises

1. Review the design of the Student Clubs database earlier in this chapter. Reviewing the lists of data types given, what data types would you assign to each of the fields in each of the tables. What lengths would you assign to the text fields?

2. Download Apache OpenOffice.org and use the database tool to open the "Student Clubs.odb" file available here. Take some time to learn how to modify the database structure and then see if you can add the required items to support the tracking of faculty advisors, as described at the end of the Normalization section in the chapter. Here is a link to the Getting Started documentation.

3. Using Microsoft Access, download the database file of comprehensive baseball statistics from the website SeanLahman.com. (If you don't have Microsoft Access, you can download an abridged version of the file here that is compatible with Apache Open Office). Review the structure of the tables included in the database. Come up with three different data-mining experiments you would like to try, and explain which fields in which tables would have to be analyzed.

4. Do some original research and find two examples of data mining. Summarize each example and then write about what the two examples have in common.

5. Conduct some independent research on the process of business intelligence. Using at least two scholarly or practitioner sources, write a two-page paper giving examples of how business intelligence is being used.

6. Conduct some independent research on the latest technologies being used for knowledge management. Using at least two scholarly or practitioner sources, write a two-page paper giving examples of software applications or new technologies being used in this field.

Chapter 5: Networking and Communication

Learning Objectives

Upon successful completion of this chapter, you will be able to:

- understand the history and development of networking technologies;
- define the key terms associated with networking technologies;
- understand the importance of broadband technologies; and
- describe organizational networking.

Introduction

In the early days of computing, computers were seen as devices for making calculations, storing data, and automating business processes. However, as the devices evolved, it became apparent that many of the functions of telecommunications could be integrated into the computer. During the 1980s, many organizations began combining their once-separate telecommunications and information-systems departments into an information technology, or IT, department. This ability for computers to communicate with one another and, maybe more importantly, to facilitate communication between individuals and groups, has been an important factor in the growth of computing over the past several decades.

Computer networking really began in the 1960s with the birth of the Internet, as we'll see below. However, while the Internet and web were evolving, corporate networking was also taking shape in the form of local area networks and client-server computing. In the 1990s, when the Internet came of age, Internet technologies began to pervade all areas of the organization. Now, with the Internet a global phenomenon, it would be unthinkable to have a computer that did not include communications capabilities. This chapter will review the different technologies that have been put in place to enable this communications revolution.

A Brief History of the Internet

In the Beginning: ARPANET

The story of the Internet, and networking in general, can be traced back to the late 1950s. The US was in the depths of the Cold War with the USSR, and each nation closely watched the other to determine which would gain a military or intelligence advantage. In 1957, the Soviets surprised the US with the launch of Sputnik, propelling us into the space age. In response to Sputnik, the US Government created the Advanced Research Projects Agency (ARPA), whose initial role was to ensure that the US was not surprised again. It was from ARPA, now called DARPA (Defense Advanced Research Projects Agency), that the Internet first sprang.

ARPA was the center of computing research in the 1960s, but there was just one problem: many of the computers could not talk to each other. In 1968, ARPA sent out a request for proposals for a communication technology that would allow different computers located around the country to be integrated together into one network. Twelve companies responded to the request, and a company named Bolt, Beranek, and Newman (BBN) won the contract. They began work right away and were able to complete the job just one year later: in September, 1969, the ARPANET was turned on. The first four nodes were at UCLA, Stanford, MIT, and the University of Utah.

The Internet and the World Wide Web

Over the next decade, the ARPANET grew and gained popularity. During this time, other networks also came into existence. Different organizations were connected to different networks. This led to a problem: the networks could not talk to each other. Each network used its own proprietary language, or protocol (see sidebar for the definition of *protocol*), to send information back and forth. This problem was solved by the invention of transmission control protocol/Internet protocol (TCP/IP). TCP/IP was designed to allow networks running on different protocols to have an intermediary protocol that would allow them to communicate. So as long as your network supported TCP/IP, you could communicate with all of the other networks running TCP/IP. TCP/IP quickly became the standard protocol and allowed networks to communicate with each other. It is from this breakthrough that we first got the term *Internet*, which simply means "an interconnected network of networks."

Sidebar: An Internet Vocabulary Lesson

Networking communication is full of some very technical concepts based on some simple principles. Learn the terms below and you'll be able to hold your own in a conversation about the Internet.

- *Packet*: The fundamental unit of data transmitted over the Internet. When a device intends to send a message to another device (for example, your PC sends a request to YouTube to open a video), it breaks the message down into smaller pieces, called packets. Each packet has the sender's address, the destination address, a sequence number, and a piece of the overall message to be sent.

- *Hub*: A simple network device that connects other devices to the network and sends packets to all the devices connected to it.

- *Bridge*: A network device that connects two networks together and only allows packets through that are needed.

- *Switch*: A network device that connects multiple devices together and filters packets based on their destination within the connected devices.

- *Router*: A device that receives and analyzes packets and then routes them towards their destination. In some cases, a router will send a packet to another router; in other cases, it will send it directly to its destination.

- *IP Address*: Every device that communicates on the Internet, whether it be a personal computer, a tablet, a smartphone, or anything else, is assigned a unique identifying number called an IP

(Internet Protocol) address. Historically, the IP-address standard used has been IPv4 (version 4), which has the format of four numbers between 0 and 255 separated by a period. For example, the domain Saylor.org has the IP address of 107.23.196.166. The IPv4 standard has a limit of 4,294,967,296 possible addresses. As the use of the Internet has proliferated, the number of IP addresses needed has grown to the point where the use of IPv4 addresses will be exhausted. This has led to the new IPv6 standard, which is currently being phased in. The IPv6 standard is formatted as eight groups of four hexadecimal digits, such as 2001:0db8:85a3:0042:1000:8a2e:0370:7334. The IPv6 standard has a limit of 3.4×10^{38} possible addresses. For more detail about the new IPv6 standard, see this Wikipedia article.

- *Domain name*: If you had to try to remember the IP address of every web server you wanted to access, the Internet would not be nearly as easy to use. A domain name is a human-friendly name for a device on the Internet. These names generally consist of a descriptive text followed by the top-level domain (TLD). For example, Wikepedia's domain name is wikipedia.org; *wikipedia* describes the organization and *.org* is the top-level domain. In this case, the *.org* TLD is designed for nonprofit organizations. Other well-known TLDs include *.com*, *.net*, and *.gov*. For a complete list and description of domain names, see this Wikipedia article.

- *DNS*: DNS stands for "domain name system," which acts as the directory on the Internet. When a request to access a device with a domain name is given, a DNS server is queried. It returns the IP address of the device requested, allowing for proper routing.

- *Packet-switching*: When a packet is sent from one device out over the Internet, it does not follow a straight path to its destination. Instead, it is passed from one router to another across the Internet until it is reaches its destination. In fact, sometimes two packets from the same message will take different routes! Sometimes, packets will arrive at their destination out of order. When this happens, the receiving device restores them to their proper order. For more details on packet-switching, see this interactive web page.

- *Protocol*: In computer networking, a protocol is the set of rules that allow two (or more) devices to exchange information back and forth across the network.

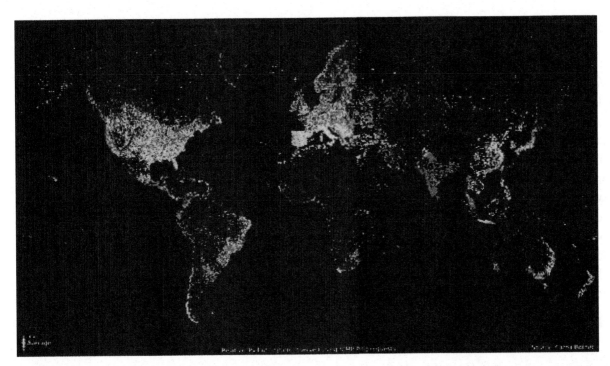

Worldwide Internet use over 24-hour period (click to go to site of origin). (Public Domain. Courtesy of the Internet Census 2012 project.)

As we moved into the 1980s, computers were added to the Internet at an increasing rate. These computers were primarily from government, academic, and research organizations. Much to the surprise of the engineers, the early popularity of the Internet was driven by the use of electronic mail (see sidebar below).

Using the Internet in these early days was not easy. In order to access information on another server, you had to know how to type in the commands necessary to access it, as well as know the name of that device. That all changed in 1990, when Tim Berners-Lee introduced his World Wide Web project, which provided an easy way to navigate the Internet through the use of linked text (hypertext). The World Wide Web gained even more steam with the release of the Mosaic browser in 1993, which allowed graphics and text to be combined together as a way to present information and navigate the Internet. The Mosaic browser took off in popularity and was soon superseded by Netscape Navigator, the first commercial web browser, in 1994. The Internet and the World Wide Web were now poised for growth. The chart below shows the growth in users from the early days until now.

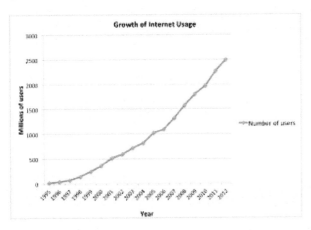

Growth of internet usage, 1995–2012 (click to enlarge). Data taken from InternetWorldStats.com.

The Dot-Com Bubble

In the 1980s and early 1990s, the Internet was being managed by the National Science Foundation (NSF). The NSF had restricted commercial ventures on the Internet, which meant that no one could buy or sell anything online. In 1991, the NSF transferred its role to three other organizations, thus getting the US government out of direct control over the Internet and essentially opening up commerce online.

This new commercialization of the Internet led to what is now known as the dot-com bubble. A frenzy of investment in new dot-com companies took place in the late 1990s, running up the stock market to new highs on a daily basis. This investment bubble was driven by the fact that investors knew that online commerce would change everything. Unfortunately, many of these new companies had poor business models and ended up with little to show for all of the funds that were invested in them. In 2000 and 2001, the bubble burst and many of these new companies went out of business. Many companies also survived, including the still-thriving Amazon (started in 1994) and eBay (1995). After the dot-com bubble burst, a new reality became clear: in order to succeed online, e-business companies would need to develop real business models and show that they could survive financially using this new technology.

Web 2.0

In the first few years of the World Wide Web, creating and putting up a website required a specific set of knowledge: you had to know how to set up a server on the World Wide Web, how to get a domain name, how to write web pages in HTML, and how to troubleshoot various technical issues as they came up. Someone who did these jobs for a website became known as a webmaster.

As the web gained in popularity, it became more and more apparent that those who did not have the skills to be a webmaster still wanted to create online content and have their own piece of the web. This need was met with new technologies that provided a website framework for those who wanted to put content online. Blogger and Wikipedia are examples of these early Web 2.0 applications, which allowed anyone with something to say a place to go and say it, without the need for understanding HTML or web-server technology.

Starting in the early 2000s, Web 2.0 applications began a second bubble of optimism and investment. It seemed that everyone wanted their own blog or photo-sharing site. Here are some of the companies that came of age during this time: MySpace (2003), Photobucket (2003), Flickr (2004), Facebook (2004), WordPress (2005), Tumblr (2006), and Twitter (2006). The ultimate indication that Web 2.0 had taken hold was when *Time* magazine named "You" its "Person of the Year" in 2006.

Sidebar: E-mail Is the "Killer" App for the Internet

When the personal computer was created, it was a great little toy for technology hobbyists and armchair programmers. As soon as the spreadsheet was invented, however, businesses took notice, and the rest is history. The spreadsheet was the killer app for the personal computer: people bought PCs just so they could run spreadsheets.

The Internet was originally designed as a way for scientists and researchers to share information and computing power among themselves. However, as soon as electronic mail was invented, it began driving demand for the Internet. This wasn't what the developers had in mind, but it turned out that people connecting to people was the killer app for the Internet.

We are seeing this again today with social networks, specifically Facebook. Many who weren't convinced to have an online presence now feel left out without a Facebook account. The connections made between people using Web 2.0 applications like Facebook on their personal computer or smartphone is driving growth yet again.

Sidebar: The Internet and the World Wide Web Are Not the Same Thing

Many times, the terms "Internet" and "World Wide Web," or even just "the web," are used interchangeably. But really, they are *not* the same thing at all! The Internet is an interconnected network of networks. Many services run across the Internet: electronic mail, voice and video, file transfers, and, yes, the World Wide Web.

The World Wide Web is simply one piece of the Internet. It is made up of web servers that have HTML pages that are being viewed on devices with web browsers. It is really that simple.

The Growth of Broadband   *Section 2.5 - 2.7*

In the early days of the Internet, most access was done via a modem over an analog telephone line. A modem (short for "modulator-demodulator") was connected to the incoming phone line and a computer in order to connect you to a network. Speeds were measured in bits-per-second (bps), with speeds growing from 1200 bps to 56,000 bps over the years. Connection to the Internet via these modems is called *dial-up* access. Dial-up was very inconvenient because it tied up the phone line. As the web became more and more interactive, dial-up also hindered usage, as users wanted to transfer more and more data. As a point of reference, downloading a typical 3.5 mb song would take 24 minutes at 1200 bps and 2 minutes at 28,800 bps.

A *broadband* connection is defined as one that has speeds of at least 256,000 bps, though most connections today are much faster, measured in millions of bits per second (megabits or mbps) or even billions (gigabits). For the home user, a broadband connection is usually accomplished via the cable television lines or phone lines (DSL). Both cable and DSL have similar prices and speeds, though each individual may find that one is better than the other for their specific area. Speeds for cable and DSL can vary during different times of the day or week, depending upon how much data traffic is being used. In more remote areas, where cable and phone companies do not provide access, home Internet connections can be made via satellite. The average home broadband speed is anywhere between 3 mbps and 30 mbps. At 10 mbps, downloading a typical 3.5 mb song would take less than a second. For businesses who require more bandwidth and reliability, telecommunications companies can provide other options, such as T1 and T3 lines.

Home Broadband vs. Dial Up, 2000-2013

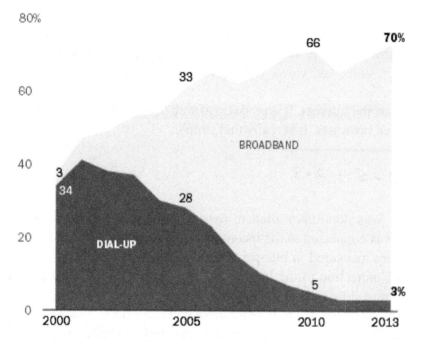

Percentage of American adults 18 years and older who access the internet via ...

Source: Pew Internet & American Life Project Surveys, March 2000-May 2013. Question wording has changed slightly over time. Our method for measuring home internet use changed in 2011, which would contribute to the seeming decline in adoption.

PEW RESEARCH CENTER

Growth of broadband use (Source: Pew Internet and American Life Project Surveys)

Broadband access is important because it impacts how the Internet is used. When a community has access to broadband, it allows them to interact more online and increases the usage of digital tools overall. Access to broadband is now considered a basic human right by the United Nations, as declared in their 2011 statement:

> "Broadband technologies are fundamentally transforming the way we live," the Broadband Commission for Digital Development, set up last year by the UN Educational Scientific and Cultural Organization (UNESCO) and the UN International Telecommunications Union (ITU), said in issuing "The Broadband Challenge" at a leadership summit in Geneva.
>
> "It is vital that no one be excluded from the new global knowledge societies we are building. We believe that communication is not just a human need – it is a right."[1]

---

1. "UN sets goal of bringing broadband to half developing world's people by 2015.", UN News Center website, http://www.un.org/apps/news/ story.asp?Cr=broadband&NewsID=40191#.Ut7JOmTTk1J

2.12 ~ 2.13 .

Wireless Networking

Today we are used to being able to access the Internet wherever we go. Our smartphones can access the Internet; Starbucks provides wireless "hotspots" for our laptops or iPads. These wireless technologies have made Internet access more convenient and have made devices such as tablets and laptops much more functional. Let's examine a few of these wireless technologies.

Wi-Fi

Wi-Fi is a technology that takes an Internet signal and converts it into radio waves. These radio waves can be picked up within a radius of approximately 65 feet by devices with a wireless adapter. Several Wi-Fi specifications have been developed over the years, starting with 802.11b (1999), followed by the 802.11g specification in 2003 and 802.11n in 2009. Each new specification improved the speed and range of Wi-Fi, allowing for more uses. One of the primary places where Wi-Fi is being used is in the home. Home users are purchasing Wi-Fi routers, connecting them to their broadband connections, and then connecting multiple devices via Wi-Fi.

Mobile Network

As the cellphone has evolved into the smartphone, the desire for Internet access on these devices has led to data networks being included as part of the mobile phone network. While Internet connections were technically available earlier, it was really with the release of the 3G networks in 2001 (2002 in the US) that smartphones and other cellular devices could access data from the Internet. This new capability drove the market for new and more powerful smartphones, such as the iPhone, introduced in 2007. In 2011, wireless carriers began offering 4G data speeds, giving the cellular networks the same speeds that customers were used to getting via their home connection.

Sidebar: Why Doesn't My Cellphone Work When I Travel Abroad?

As mobile phone technologies have evolved, providers in different countries have chosen different communication standards for their mobile phone networks. In the US, both of the two competing standards exist: GSM (used by AT&T and T-Mobile) and CDMA (used by the other major carriers). Each standard has its pros and cons, but the bottom line is that phones using one standard cannot easily switch to the other. In the US, this is not a big deal because mobile networks exist to support both standards. But when you travel to other countries, you will find that most of them use GSM networks, with the one big exception being Japan, which has standardized on CDMA. It is possible for a mobile phone using one type of network to switch to the other type of network by switching out the SIM card, which controls your access to the mobile network. However, this will not work in all cases. If you are traveling abroad, it is always best to consult with your mobile provider to determine the best way to access a mobile network.

2.9 - 2.11

Bluetooth

While Bluetooth is not generally used to connect a device to the Internet, it is an important wireless technology that has enabled many functionalities that are used every day. When created in 1994 by Ericsson, it was intended to replace wired connections between devices. Today, it is the standard method for connecting nearby devices wirelessly. Bluetooth has a range of approximately 300 feet and consumes very little power, making it an excellent choice for a variety of purposes. Some applications of Bluetooth include: connecting a printer to a personal computer, connecting a mobile phone and headset, connecting a wireless keyboard and mouse to a computer, and connecting a remote for a presentation made on a personal computer.

VoIP

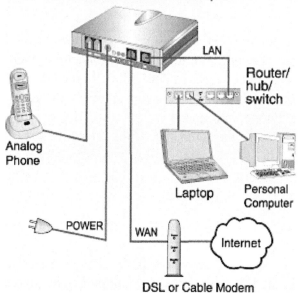

A typical VoIP communication. Image courtesy of BroadVoice.

A growing class of data being transferred over the Internet is voice data. A protocol called voice over IP, or VoIP, enables sounds to be converted to a digital format for transmission over the Internet and then re-created at the other end. By using many existing technologies and software, voice communication over the Internet is now available to anyone with a browser (think Skype, Google Hangouts). Beyond this, many companies are now offering VoIP-based telephone service for business and home use.

Organizational Networking

LAN and WAN

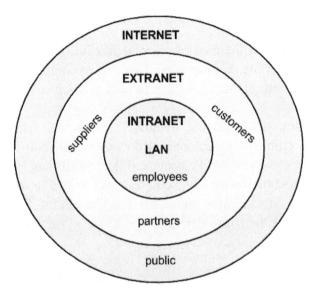

Scope of business networks

While the Internet was evolving and creating a way for organizations to connect to each other and the world, another revolution was taking place inside organizations. The proliferation of personal computers inside organizations led to the need to share resources such as printers, scanners, and data. Organizations solved this problem through the creation of local area networks (LANs), which allowed computers to connect to each other and to peripherals. These same networks also allowed personal computers to hook up to legacy mainframe computers.

An LAN is (by definition) a local network, usually operating in the same building or on the same campus. When an organization needed to provide a network over a wider area (with locations in different cities or states, for example), they would build a wide area network (WAN).

Client-Server

The personal computer originally was used as a stand-alone computing device. A program was installed on the computer and then used to do word processing or number crunching. However, with the advent of networking and local area networks, computers could work together to solve problems. Higher-end computers were installed as servers, and users on the local network could run applications and share information among departments and organizations. This is called client-server computing.

Intranet

Just as organizations set up web sites to provide global access to information about their business, they also set up internal web pages to provide information about the organization to the employees. This internal set of web pages is called an intranet. Web pages on the intranet are not accessible to those outside the company; in fact, those pages would come up as "not found" if an employee tried to access them from outside the company's network.

Extranet

Sometimes an organization wants to be able to collaborate with its customers or suppliers while at the same time maintaining the security of being inside its own network. In cases like this a company may want to create an *extranet*, which is a part of the company's network that can be made available securely to those outside of the company. Extranets can be used to allow customers to log in and check the status of their orders, or for suppliers to check their customers' inventory levels.

Sometimes, an organization will need to allow someone who is not located physically within its internal network to gain access. This access can be provided by a virtual private network (VPN). VPNs will be discussed further in the chapter 6 (on information security).

Sidebar: Microsoft's SharePoint Powers the Intranet

As organizations begin to see the power of collaboration between their employees, they often look for solutions that will allow them to leverage their intranet to enable more collaboration. Since most companies use Microsoft products for much of their computing, it is only natural that they have looked to Microsoft to provide a solution. This solution is Microsoft's SharePoint.

SharePoint provides a communication and collaboration platform that integrates seamlessly with Microsoft's Office suite of applications. Using SharePoint, employees can share a document and edit it together – no more e-mailing that Word document to everyone for review. Projects and documents can be managed collaboratively across the organization. Corporate documents are indexed and made available for search. No more asking around for that procedures document – now you just search for it in SharePoint. For organizations looking to add a social networking component to their intranet, Microsoft offers Yammer, which can be used by itself or integrated into SharePoint.

Cloud Computing

We covered cloud computing in chapter 3, but it should also be mentioned here. The universal availability of the Internet combined with increases in processing power and data-storage capacity have made cloud computing a viable option for many companies. Using cloud computing, companies or individuals can contract to store data on storage devices somewhere on the Internet. Applications can be "rented" as needed, giving a company the ability to quickly deploy new applications. You can read about cloud computing in more detail in chapter 3.

Sidebar: Metcalfe's Law

Just as Moore's Law describes how computing power is increasing over time, Metcalfe's Law describes the power of networking. Specifically, Metcalfe's Law states that the value of a telecommunications network is proportional to the square of the number of connected users of the system. Think about it this way: If none of your friends were on Facebook, would you spend much time there? If no one else at your school or place of work had e-mail, would it be very useful to you? Metcalfe's Law tries to quantify this value.

Summary

The networking revolution has completely changed how the computer is used. Today, no one would imagine using a computer that was not connected to one or more networks. The development of the Internet and World Wide Web, combined with wireless access, has made information available at our fingertips. The Web 2.0 revolution has made us all authors of web content. As networking technology has matured, the use of Internet technologies has become a standard for every type of organization. The use of intranets and extranets has allowed organizations to deploy functionality to employees and business partners alike, increasing efficiencies and improving communications. Cloud computing has truly made information available everywhere and has serious implications for the role of the IT department.

Study Questions

1. What were the first four locations hooked up to the Internet (ARPANET)?
2. What does the term *packet* mean?
3. Which came first, the Internet or the World Wide Web?
4. What was revolutionary about Web 2.0?
5. What was the so-called killer app for the Internet?
6. What makes a connection a *broadband* connection?
7. What does the term VoIP mean?
8. What is an LAN?
9. What is the difference between an intranet and an extranet?
10. What is Metcalfe's Law?

Exercises

1. What is the IP address of your computer? How did you find out? What is the IP address of google.com? How did you find out? Did you get IPv4 or IPv6 addresses?
2. What is the difference between the Internet and the World Wide Web? Create at least three statements that identify the differences between the two.
3. Who are the broadband providers in your area? What are the prices and speeds offered?
4. Pretend you are planning a trip to three foreign countries in the next month. Consult your wireless carrier to determine if your mobile phone would work properly in those countries. What would the costs be? What alternatives do you have if it would not work?

Chapter 6: Information Systems Security

David T. Bourgeois

Learning Objectives

Upon successful completion of this chapter, you will be able to:

- identify the information security triad;
- identify and understand the high-level concepts surrounding information security tools; and
- secure yourself digitally.

Introduction

As computers and other digital devices have become essential to business and commerce, they have also increasingly become a target for attacks. In order for a company or an individual to use a computing device with confidence, they must first be assured that the device is not compromised in any way and that all communications will be secure. In this chapter, we will review the fundamental concepts of information systems security and discuss some of the measures that can be taken to mitigate security threats. We will begin with an overview focusing on how organizations can stay secure. Several different measures that a company can take to improve security will be discussed. We will then follow up by reviewing security precautions that individuals can take in order to secure their personal computing environment.

The security triad

The Information Security Triad: Confidentiality, Integrity, Availability (CIA)

Confidentiality

When protecting information, we want to be able to restrict access to those who are allowed to see it; everyone else should be disallowed from learning anything about its contents. This is the essence of confidentiality. For example, federal law requires that universities restrict access to private student information. The university must be sure that only those who are authorized have access to view the grade records.

Integrity

Integrity is the assurance that the information being accessed has not been altered and truly represents what is intended. Just as a person with integrity means what he or she says and can be trusted to consistently represent the truth, information integrity means information truly represents its intended meaning. Information can lose its integrity through malicious intent, such as when someone who is not authorized makes a change to intentionally misrepresent something. An example of this would be when a hacker is hired to go into the university's system and change a grade.

Integrity can also be lost unintentionally, such as when a computer power surge corrupts a file or someone authorized to make a change accidentally deletes a file or enters incorrect information.

Availability

Information availability is the third part of the CIA triad. *Availability* means that information can be accessed and modified by anyone authorized to do so in an appropriate timeframe. Depending on the type of information, *appropriate timeframe* can mean different things. For example, a stock trader needs information to be available immediately, while a sales person may be happy to get sales numbers for the day in a report the next morning. Companies such as Amazon.com will require their servers to be available twenty-four hours a day, seven days a week. Other companies may not suffer if their web servers are down for a few minutes once in a while.

Tools for Information Security

In order to ensure the confidentiality, integrity, and availability of information, organizations can choose from a variety of tools. Each of these tools can be utilized as part of an overall information-security policy, which will be discussed in the next section.

Authentication

The most common way to identify someone is through their physical appearance, but how do we identify someone sitting behind a computer screen or at the ATM? Tools for authentication are used to ensure that the person accessing the information is, indeed, who they present themselves to be.

Authentication can be accomplished by identifying someone through one or more of three factors: something they know, something they have, or something they are. For example, the most common form of authentication today is the user ID and password. In this case, the authentication is done by confirming something that the user knows (their ID and password). But this form of authentication is easy to compromise (see sidebar) and stronger forms of authentication are sometimes needed. Identifying someone only by something they have, such as a key or a card, can also be problematic. When that identifying token is lost or stolen, the identity can be easily stolen. The final factor, something you are, is much harder to compromise. This factor identifies a user through the use of a physical characteristic, such as an eye-scan or fingerprint. Identifying someone through their physical characteristics is called biometrics.

A more secure way to authenticate a user is to do multi-factor authentication. By combining two or more of the factors listed above, it becomes much more difficult for someone to misrepresent themselves. An example of this would be the use of an RSA SecurID token. The RSA device is something you have, and will generate a new access code every sixty seconds. To log in to an information resource using the RSA device, you combine something you know, a four-digit PIN, with the code generated by the device. The only way to properly authenticate is by both knowing the code *and* having the RSA device.

Access Control

Once a user has been authenticated, the next step is to ensure that they can only access the information resources that are appropriate. This is done through the use of access control. Access control determines which users are authorized to read, modify, add, and/or delete information. Several different access control models exist. Here we will discuss two: the access control list (ACL) and role-based access control (RBAC).

For each information resource that an organization wishes to manage, a list of users who have the ability to take specific actions can be created. This is an access control list, or ACL. For each user, specific capabilities are assigned, such as *read*, *write*, *delete*, or *add*. Only users with those capabilities are allowed to perform those functions. If a user is not on the list, they have no ability to even know that the information resource exists.

ACLs are simple to understand and maintain. However, they have several drawbacks. The primary drawback is that each information resource is managed separately, so if a security administrator wanted to add or remove a user to a large set of information resources, it would be quite difficult. And as the number of users and resources increase, ACLs become harder to maintain. This has led to an improved method of access control, called role-based access control, or RBAC. With RBAC, instead of giving specific users access rights to an information resource, users are assigned to roles and then those roles are assigned the access. This allows the administrators to manage users and roles separately, simplifying administration and, by extension, improving security.

Access Control List

User	Read	Write	Add	Delete
jsmith	x			
rlee	x			
knguyen	x	x	x	x
mroberts	x	x		
manderson	x	x		

Role-Based Access Control

Role	Read	Write	Add	Delete
Reader	x			
Editor	x	x		
Administrato	x	x	x	x

Role Assignments

User	Role
jsmith	Reader
rlee	Reader
knguyen	Admin
mroberts	Editor
manderson	Editor

Comparison of ACL and RBAC (click to enlarge)

Encryption

Many times, an organization needs to transmit information over the Internet or transfer it on external media such as a CD or flash drive. In these cases, even with proper authentication and access control, it is possible for an unauthorized person to get access to the data. Encryption is a process of encoding data upon its transmission or storage so that only authorized individuals can read it. This encoding is accomplished by a computer program, which encodes the plain text that needs to be transmitted; then the recipient receives the cipher text and decodes it (decryption). In order for this to work, the sender and receiver need to agree on the method of encoding so that both parties can communicate properly. Both parties share the encryption key, enabling them to encode and decode each other's messages. This is called symmetric key encryption. This type of encryption is problematic because the key is available in two different places.

An alternative to symmetric key encryption is public key encryption. In public key encryption, two keys are used: a public key and a private key. To send an encrypted message, you obtain the public key, encode the message, and send it. The recipient then uses the private key to decode it. The public key can be given to anyone who wishes to send the recipient a message. Each user simply needs one private key and one public key in order to secure messages. The private key is necessary in order to decrypt something sent with the public key.

Public Key Encryption Example

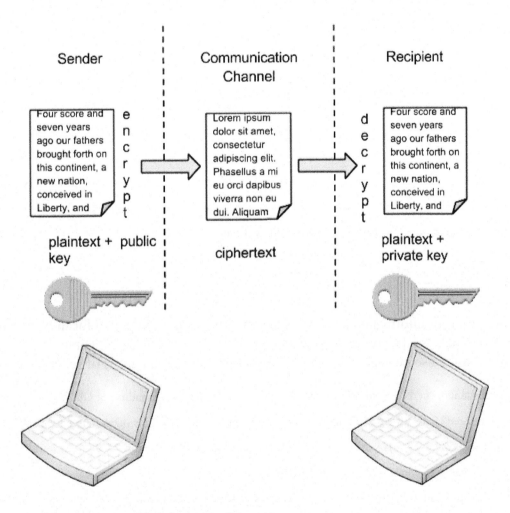

Public key encryption (click for larger diagram)

Sidebar: Password Security

So why is using just a simple user ID/password not considered a secure method of authentication? It turns out that this single-factor authentication is extremely easy to compromise. Good password policies must be put in place in order to ensure that passwords cannot be compromised. Below are some of the more common policies that organizations should put in place.

- Require complex passwords. One reason passwords are compromised is that they can be easily guessed. A recent study found that the top three passwords people used in 2012 were *password*, *123456* and *12345678*.[1] A password should not be simple, or a word that can be found in a dictionary. One of the first things a hacker will do is try to crack a password

---

1. "Born to be breached" by Sean Gallagher on Nov 3 2012. *Arstechnica*. Retrieved from http://arstechnica.com/information-technology/2012/11/born-to-be-breached-the-worst-passwords-are-still-the-most-common/ on May 15, 2013.

by testing every term in the dictionary! Instead, a good password policy is one that requires the use of a minimum of eight characters, and at least one upper-case letter, one special character, and one number.

- Change passwords regularly. It is essential that users change their passwords on a regular basis. Users should change their passwords every sixty to ninety days, ensuring that any passwords that might have been stolen or guessed will not be able to be used against the company.

- Train employees not to give away passwords. One of the primary methods that is used to steal passwords is to simply figure them out by asking the users or administrators. *Pretexting* occurs when an attacker calls a helpdesk or security administrator and pretends to be a particular authorized user having trouble logging in. Then, by providing some personal information about the authorized user, the attacker convinces the security person to reset the password and tell him what it is. Another way that employees may be tricked into giving away passwords is through e-mail phishing. Phishing occurs when a user receives an e-mail that looks as if it is from a trusted source, such as their bank, or their employer. In the e-mail, the user is asked to click a link and log in to a website that mimics the genuine website and enter their ID and password, which are then captured by the attacker.

Backups

Another essential tool for information security is a comprehensive backup plan for the entire organization. Not only should the data on the corporate servers be backed up, but individual computers used throughout the organization should also be backed up. A good backup plan should consist of several components.

- A full understanding of the organizational information resources. What information does the organization actually have? Where is it stored? Some data may be stored on the organization's servers, other data on users' hard drives, some in the cloud, and some on third-party sites. An organization should make a full inventory of all of the information that needs to be backed up and determine the best way back it up.

- Regular backups of all data. The frequency of backups should be based on how important the data is to the company, combined with the ability of the company to replace any data that is lost. Critical data should be backed up daily, while less critical data could be backed up weekly.

- Offsite storage of backup data sets. If all of the backup data is being stored in the same facility as the original copies of the data, then a single event, such as an earthquake, fire, or tornado, would take out both the original data and the backup! It is essential that part of the backup plan is to store the data in an offsite location.

- Test of data restoration. On a regular basis, the backups should be put to the test by having some of the data restored. This will ensure that the process is working and will give the organization confidence in the backup plan.

Besides these considerations, organizations should also examine their operations to determine what effect downtime would have on their business. If their information technology were to be unavailable for any sustained period of time, how would it impact the business?

Additional concepts related to backup include the following:

- Universal Power Supply (UPS). A UPS is a device that provides battery backup to critical components of the system, allowing them to stay online longer and/or allowing the IT staff to shut them down using proper procedures in order to prevent the data loss that might occur from a power failure.
- Alternate, or "hot" sites. Some organizations choose to have an alternate site where an exact replica of their critical data is always kept up to date. When the primary site goes down, the alternate site is immediately brought online so that little or no downtime is experienced.

As information has become a strategic asset, a whole industry has sprung up around the technologies necessary for implementing a proper backup strategy. A company can contract with a service provider to back up all of their data or they can purchase large amounts of online storage space and do it themselves. Technologies such as storage area networks and archival systems are now used by most large businesses.

Firewalls

Another method that an organization should use to increase security on its network is a firewall. A firewall can exist as hardware or software (or both). A hardware firewall is a device that is connected to the network and filters the packets based on a set of rules. A software firewall runs on the operating system and intercepts packets as they arrive to a computer. A firewall protects all company servers and computers by stopping packets from outside the organization's network that do not meet a strict set of criteria. A firewall may also be configured to restrict the flow of packets leaving the organization. This may be done to eliminate the possibility of employees watching YouTube videos or using Facebook from a company computer.

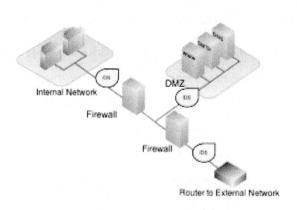

Network configuration with firewalls, IDS, and a DMZ. Click to enlarge.

Some organizations may choose to implement multiple firewalls as part of their network security configuration, creating one or more sections of their network that are partially secured. This segment of the network is referred to as a DMZ, borrowing the term *demilitarized zone* from the military, and it is where an organization may place resources that need broader access but still need to be secured.

Intrusion Detection Systems

Another device that can be placed on the network for security purposes is an intrusion detection system, or IDS. An IDS does not add any additional security; instead, it provides the functionality to identify if the network is being attacked. An IDS can be configured to watch for specific types of activities and then alert security personnel if that activity occurs. An IDS also can log various types of traffic on the network for analysis later. An IDS is an essential part of any good security setup.

Sidebar: Virtual Private Networks

Using firewalls and other security technologies, organizations can effectively protect many of their information resources by making them invisible to the outside world. But what if an employee working from home requires access to some of these resources? What if a consultant is hired who needs to do work on the internal corporate network from a remote location? In these cases, a virtual private network (VPN) is called for.

A VPN allows a user who is outside of a corporate network to take a detour around the firewall and access the internal network from the outside. Through a combination of software and security measures, this lets an organization allow limited access to its networks while at the same time ensuring overall security.

Physical Security

An organization can implement the best authentication scheme in the world, develop the best access control, and install firewalls and intrusion prevention, but its security cannot be complete without implementation of physical security. Physical security is the protection of the actual hardware and networking components that store and transmit information resources. To implement physical security, an organization must identify all of the vulnerable resources and take measures to ensure that these resources cannot be physically tampered with or stolen. These measures include the following.

- Locked doors: It may seem obvious, but all the security in the world is useless if an intruder can simply walk in and physically remove a computing device. High-value information assets should be secured in a location with limited access.

- Physical intrusion detection: High-value information assets should be monitored through the use of security cameras and other means to detect unauthorized access to the physical locations where they exist.

- Secured equipment: Devices should be locked down to prevent them from being stolen. One employee's hard drive could contain all of your customer information, so it is essential that it be secured.

- Environmental monitoring: An organization's servers and other high-value equipment should always be kept in a room that is monitored for temperature, humidity, and airflow. The risk of a server failure rises when these factors go out of a specified range.

- Employee training: One of the most common ways thieves steal corporate information is to steal employee laptops while employees are traveling. Employees should be trained to secure their equipment whenever they are away from the office.

Security Policies

Besides the technical controls listed above, organizations also need to implement security policies as a form of administrative control. In fact, these policies should really be a starting point in developing an overall security plan. A good information-security policy lays out the guidelines for employee use of the information resources of the company and provides the company recourse in the case that an employee violates a policy.

According to the SANS Institute, a good policy is "a formal, brief, and high-level statement or plan that embraces an organization's general beliefs, goals, objectives, and acceptable procedures for a specified subject area." Policies require compliance; failure to comply with a policy will result in disciplinary action. A policy does not lay out the specific technical details, instead it focuses on the desired results. A security policy should be based on the guiding principles of confidentiality, integrity, and availability.[2]

A good example of a security policy that many will be familiar with is a web use policy. A web use policy lays out the responsibilities of company employees as they use company resources to access the Internet. A good example of a web use policy is included in Harvard University's "Computer Rules and Responsibilities" policy, which can be found here.

A security policy should also address any governmental or industry regulations that apply to the organization. For example, if the organization is a university, it must be aware of the Family Educational Rights and Privacy Act (FERPA), which restricts who has access to student information. Health care organizations are obligated to follow several regulations, such as the Health Insurance Portability and Accountability Act (HIPAA).

A good resource for learning more about security policies is the SANS Institute's Information Security Policy Page.

Sidebar: Mobile Security

As the use of mobile devices such as smartphones and tablets proliferates, organizations must be ready to address the unique security concerns that the use of these devices bring. One of the first questions an organization must consider is whether to allow mobile devices in the workplace at all. Many employees already have these devices, so the question becomes: Should we allow employees to bring their own devices and use them as part of their employment activities? Or should we provide the devices to our employees? Creating a BYOD ("Bring Your Own Device") policy allows employees to integrate themselves more fully into their job and can bring higher employee satisfaction and productivity. In many cases, it may be virtually impossible to prevent employees from having their own smartphones or iPads in the workplace. If the organization provides the devices to its employees, it gains more control over use of the devices, but it also exposes itself to the possibility of an administrative (and costly) mess.

Mobile devices can pose many unique security challenges to an organization. Probably one of the biggest concerns is theft of intellectual property. For an employee with malicious intent, it would be a very simple process to connect a mobile device either to a computer via the USB port, or wirelessly to the corporate network, and download confidential data. It would also be easy to secretly take a high-quality picture using a built-in camera.

When an employee does have permission to access and save company data on his or her device, a different security threat emerges: that device now becomes a target for thieves. Theft of mobile devices (in this case, including laptops) is one of the primary methods that data thieves use.

So what can be done to secure mobile devices? It will start with a good policy regarding their use. According to a 2013 SANS study, organizations should consider developing a mobile device policy that addresses the following issues: use of the camera, use of voice recording, application purchases, encryption at rest, Wi-Fi autoconnect settings, bluetooth settings, VPN use, password settings, lost or stolen device reporting, and backup.[3]

---

2. SANS Institute. "A Short Primer for Developing Security Policies." Accessed from http://www.sans.org/security-resources/policies/Policy_Primer.pdf on May 31, 2013.

Besides policies, there are several different tools that an organization can use to mitigate some of these risks. For example, if a device is stolen or lost, geolocation software can help the organization find it. In some cases, it may even make sense to install remote data-removal software, which will remove data from a device if it becomes a security risk.

Usability

When looking to secure information resources, organizations must balance the need for security with users' need to effectively access and use these resources. If a system's security measures make it difficult to use, then users will find ways around the security, which may make the system more vulnerable than it would have been without the security measures! Take, for example, password policies. If the organization requires an extremely long password with several special characters, an employee may resort to writing it down and putting it in a drawer since it will be impossible to memorize.

Personal Information Security

We will end this chapter with a discussion of what measures each of us, as individual users, can take to secure our computing technologies. There is no way to have 100% security, but there are several simple steps we, as individuals, can take to make ourselves more secure.

Poster from Stop. Think. Connect. Click to enlarge. (Copyright: Stop. Think. Connect. http://stopthinkconnect.org/resources)

- Keep your software up to date. Whenever a software vendor determines that a security flaw has been found in their software, they will release an update to the software that you can download to fix the problem. Turn on automatic updating on your computer to automate this process.

- Install antivirus software and keep it up to date. There are many good antivirus software packages on the market today, including free ones.

- Be smart about your connections. You should be aware of your surroundings. When connecting to a Wi-Fi network in a public place, be aware that you could be at risk of being spied on by others sharing that network. It is advisable not to access your financial or personal data while attached to a Wi-Fi hotspot. You should also be aware that connecting USB flash drives to your device could also put you at risk. Do not attach an unfamiliar flash drive to your device unless you can scan it first with your security software.

- Back up your data. Just as organizations need to back up their data, individuals need to as well. And the same rules apply: do it regularly and keep a copy of it in another location. One simple solution for this is to set up an account with an online backup service, such as Mozy or Carbonite, to automate your backups.

---

3. Taken from SANS Institute's Mobile Device Checklist. You can review the full checklist at www.sans.org/score/checklists/mobile-device-checklist.xls.

- Secure your accounts with two-factor authentication. Most e-mail and social media providers now have a two-factor authentication option. The way this works is simple: when you log in to your account from an unfamiliar computer for the first time, it sends you a text message with a code that you must enter to confirm that you are really you. This means that no one else can log in to your accounts without knowing your password *and* having your mobile phone with them.

- Make your passwords long, strong, and unique. For your personal passwords, you should follow the same rules that are recommended for organizations. Your passwords should be long (eight or more characters) and contain at least two of the following: upper-case letters, numbers, and special characters. You also should use different passwords for different accounts, so that if someone steals your password for one account, they still are locked out of your other accounts.

- Be suspicious of strange links and attachments. When you receive an e-mail, tweet, or Facebook post, be suspicious of any links or attachments included there. Do not click on the link directly if you are at all suspicious. Instead, if you want to access the website, find it yourself and navigate to it directly.

You can find more about these steps and many other ways to be secure with your computing by going to Stop. Think. Connect. This website is part of a campaign that was launched in October of 2010 by the STOP. THINK. CONNECT. Messaging Convention in partnership with the U.S. government, including the White House.

Summary

As computing and networking resources have become more and more an integral part of business, they have also become a target of criminals. Organizations must be vigilant with the way they protect their resources. The same holds true for us personally: as digital devices become more and more intertwined with our lives, it becomes crucial for us to understand how to protect ourselves.

Study Questions

1. Briefly define each of the three members of the information security triad.
2. What does the term *authentication* mean?
3. What is multi-factor authentication?
4. What is role-based access control?
5. What is the purpose of encryption?
6. What are two good examples of a complex password?
7. What is pretexting?
8. What are the components of a good backup plan?
9. What is a firewall?
10. What does the term *physical security* mean?

Exercises

1. Describe one method of multi-factor authentication that you have experienced and discuss the pros and cons of using multi-factor authentication.

2. What are some of the latest advances in encryption technologies? Conduct some independent research on encryption using scholarly or practitioner resources, then write a two- to three-page paper that describes at least two new advances in encryption technology.

3. What is the password policy at your place of employment or study? Do you have to change passwords every so often? What are the minimum requirements for a password?

4. When was the last time you backed up your data? What method did you use? In one to two pages, describe a method for backing up your data. Ask your instructor if you can get extra credit for backing up your data.

5. Find the information security policy at your place of employment or study. Is it a good policy? Does it meet the standards outlined in the chapter?

6. How are you doing on keeping your own information secure? Review the steps listed in the chapter and comment on how well you are doing.

Part 2: Information Systems for Strategic Advantage

Chapter 7: Does IT Matter?

Learning Objectives

Upon successful completion of this chapter, you will be able to:

- define the productivity paradox and explain the current thinking on this topic;
- evaluate Carr's argument in "Does IT Matter?";
- describe the components of competitive advantage; and
- describe information systems that can provide businesses with competitive advantage.

Introduction

For over fifty years, computing technology has been a part of business. Organizations have spent trillions of dollars on information technologies. But has all this investment in IT made a difference? Have we seen increases in productivity? Are companies that invest in IT more competitive? In this chapter, we will look at the value IT can bring to an organization and try to answer these questions. We will begin by highlighting two important works from the past two decades.

The Productivity Paradox

In 1991, Erik Brynjolfsson wrote an article, published in the *Communications of the ACM*, entitled "The Productivity Paradox of Information Technology: Review and Assessment." By reviewing studies about the impact of IT investment on productivity, Brynjolfsson was able to conclude that the addition of information technology to business had not improved productivity at all – the "productivity paradox." From the article[1] He does not draw any specific conclusions from this finding, and provides the following analysis:

> Although it is too early to conclude that IT's productivity contribution has been subpar, a paradox remains in our inability to unequivocally document any contribution after so much effort. The various explanations that have been proposed can be grouped into four categories:
> **1) Mismeasurement** of outputs and inputs,
> **2) Lags** due to learning and adjustment,
> **3) Redistribution** and dissipation of profits,
> **4) Mismanagement** of information and technology.

1. Brynjolfsson, Erik. "The Productivity Paradox of Information Technology: Review and Assessment" Copyright © 1993, 1994 Erik Brynjolfsson, All Rights Reserved Center for Coordination Science MIT Sloan School of Management Cambridge, Massachusetts Previous version: December 1991 This Version: September 1992 Published in Communications of the ACM, December, 1993; and Japan Management Research, June, 1994 (in Japanese).

In 1998, Brynjolfsson and Lorin Hitt published a follow-up paper entitled "Beyond the Productivity Paradox."[2] In this paper, the authors utilized new data that had been collected and found that IT did, indeed, provide a positive result for businesses. Further, they found that sometimes the true advantages in using technology were not directly relatable to higher productivity, but to "softer" measures, such as the impact on organizational structure. They also found that the impact of information technology can vary widely between companies.

IT Doesn't Matter

Just as a consensus was forming about the value of IT, the Internet stock market bubble burst. Just two years later, in 2003, Harvard professor Nicholas Carr wrote his article "IT Doesn't Matter" in the *Harvard Business Review*. In this article Carr asserts that as information technology has become more ubiquitous, it has also become less of a differentiator. In other words: because information technology is so readily available and the software used so easily copied, businesses cannot hope to implement these tools to provide any sort of competitive advantage. Carr goes on to suggest that since IT is essentially a commodity, it should be managed like one: low cost, low risk. Using the analogy of electricity, Carr describes how a firm should never be the first to try a new technology, thereby letting others take the risks. IT management should see themselves as a utility within the company and work to keep costs down . For IT, providing the best service with minimal downtime is the goal.

As you can imagine, this article caused quite an uproar, especially from IT companies. Many articles were written in defense of IT; many others in support of Carr. Carr released a book based on the article in 2004, entitled *Does IT Matter?* Click here to watch a video of Carr being interviewed about his book on CNET.

Probably the best thing to come out of the article and subsequent book was that it opened up discussion on the place of IT in a business strategy, and exactly what role IT could play in competitive advantage. It is that question that we want to address in the rest of the this chapter.

[Embed "IT Doesn't Matter" classroom video footage here: http://quickstream.biola.edu/distancelearning/busn220bourgeois/ITDoesn'tMatter.f4v]

Competitive Advantage

What does it mean when a company has a competitive advantage? What are the factors that play into it? While there are entire courses and many different opinions on this topic, let's go with one of the most accepted definitions, developed by Michael Porter in his book *Competitive Advantage: Creating and Sustaining Superior Performance*. A company is said to have a competitive advantage over its rivals when it is able to sustain profits that exceed average for the industry. According to Porter, there are two primary methods for obtaining competitive advantage: cost advantage and differentiation advantage. So the question becomes: how can information technology be a factor in one or both of these methods? In the sections below we will explore this question using two of Porter's analysis tools: the value chain and the five forces model. We will also use Porter's analysis in his 2001 article "Strategy and the Internet," which examines the impact of the Internet on business strategy and competitive advantage, to shed further light on the role of information technology in competitive advantage.

---

2. Brynjolfsson, Erik and Lorin Hitt. "Beyond the Productivity Paradox", Communications of the ACM, August 1998, Vol. 41(8): pp. 49–55. Copyright © 1998 by Association for Computing Machinery, Inc. (ACM).

The Value Chain

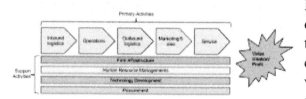

Porter's value chain (click to enlarge)

In his book, Porter describes exactly how a company can create value (and therefore profit). Value is built through the value chain: a series of activities undertaken by the company to produce a product or service. Each step in the value chain contributes to the overall value of a product or service. While the value chain may not be a perfect model for every type of company, it does provide a way to analyze just how a company is producing value. The value chain is made up of two sets of activities: primary activities and support activities. We will briefly examine these activities and discuss how information technology can play a role in creating value by contributing to cost advantage or differentiation advantage, or both.

The primary activities are the functions that directly impact the creation of a product or service. The goal of the primary activities is to add more value than they cost. The primary activities are:

- Inbound logistics: These are the functions performed to bring in raw materials and other needed inputs. Information technology can be used here to make these processes more efficient, such as with supply-chain management systems, which allow the suppliers to manage their own inventory.

- Operations: Any part of a business that is involved in converting the raw materials into the final products or services is part of operations. From manufacturing to business process management (covered in chapter 8), information technology can be used to provide more efficient processes and increase innovation through flows of information.

- Outbound logistics: These are the functions required to get the product out to the customer. As with inbound logistics, IT can be used here to improve processes, such as allowing for real-time inventory checks. IT can also be a delivery mechanism itself.

- Sales/Marketing: The functions that will entice buyers to purchase the products are part of sales and marketing. Information technology is used in almost all aspects of this activity. From online advertising to online surveys, IT can be used to innovate product design and reach customers like never before. The company website can be a sales channel itself.

- Service: The functions a business performs after the product has been purchased to maintain and enhance the product's value are part of the service activity. Service can be enhanced via technology as well, including support services through websites and knowledge bases.

The support activities are the functions in an organization that support, and cut across, all of the primary activities. The support activities are:

- Firm infrastructure: This includes organizational functions such as finance, accounting, and quality control, all of which depend on information technology; the use of ERP systems (to be covered in chapter 9) is a good example of the impact that IT can have on these functions.

- Human resource management: This activity consists of recruiting, hiring, and other services needed to attract and retain employees. Using the Internet, HR departments can increase their reach when looking for candidates. There is also the possibility of allowing employees to use technology for a more flexible work environment.

- Technology development: Here we have the technological advances and innovations that support the primary activities. These advances are then integrated across the firm or within one of the primary activities to add value. Information technology would fall specifically under this activity.

- Procurement: The activities involved in acquiring the raw materials used in the creation of products and services are called procurement. Business-to-business e-commerce can be used to improve the acquisition of materials.

This analysis of the value chain provides some insight into how information technology can lead to competitive advantage. Let's now look at another tool that Porter developed – the "five forces" model.

Porter's Five Forces

Porter developed the "five forces" model as a framework for industry analysis. This model can be used to help understand just how competitive an industry is and to analyze its strengths and weaknesses. The model consists of five elements, each of which plays a role in determining the average profitability of an industry. In 2001, Porter wrote an article entitled "Strategy and the Internet," in which he takes this model and looks at how the Internet impacts the profitability of an industry. Below is a quick summary of each of the five forces and the impact of the Internet.

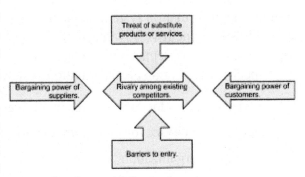

Porter's five forces (click to enlarge)

- **Threat of substitute products or services:** How easily can a product or service be replaced with something else? The more types of products or services there are that can meet a particular need, the less profitability there will be in an industry. For example, the advent of the mobile phone has replaced the need for pagers. The Internet has made people more aware of substitute products, driving down industry profits in those industries being substituted.

- **Bargaining power of suppliers:** When a company has several suppliers to choose from, it can demand a lower price. When a sole supplier exists, then the company is at the mercy of the supplier. For example, if only one company makes the controller chip for a car engine, that company can control the price, at least to some extent. The Internet has given companies access to more suppliers, driving down prices. On the other hand, suppliers now also have the ability to sell directly to customers.

- **Bargaining power of customers:** A company that is the sole provider of a unique product has the ability to control pricing. But the Internet has given customers many more options to choose from.

- **Barriers to entry:** The easier it is to enter an industry, the tougher it will be to make a profit in that industry. The Internet has an overall effect of making it easier to enter industries. It is also very easy to copy technology, so new innovations will not last that long.
- **Rivalry among existing competitors:** The more competitors there are in an industry, the bigger a factor price becomes. The advent of the Internet has increased competition by widening the geographic market and lowering the costs of doing business. For example, a manufacturer in Southern California may now have to compete against a manufacturer in the South, where wages are lower.

Porter's five forces are used to analyze an industry to determine the average profitability of a company within that industry. Adding in Porter's analysis of the Internet, we can see that the Internet (and by extension, information technology in general) has the effect of lowering overall profitability. [3] While the Internet has certainly produced many companies that are big winners, the overall winners have been the consumers, who have been given an ever-increasing market of products and services and lower prices.

Using Information Systems for Competitive Advantage

Now that we have an understanding of competitive advantage and some of the ways that IT may be used to help organizations gain it, we will turn our attention to some specific examples. A strategic information system is an information system that is designed specifically to implement an organizational strategy meant to provide a competitive advantage. These sorts of systems began popping up in the 1980s, as noted in a paper by Charles Wiseman entitled "Creating Competitive Weapons From Information Systems."[4]
Specifically, a strategic information system is one that attempts to do one or more of the following:

- deliver a product or a service at a lower cost;
- deliver a product or service that is differentiated;
- help an organization focus on a specific market segment;
- enable innovation.

Following are some examples of information systems that fall into this category.

Business Process Management Systems

In their book, *IT Doesn't Matter – Business Processes Do*, Howard Smith and Peter Fingar argue that it is the integration of information systems with business processes that leads to competitive advantage. They then go on to state that Carr's article is dangerous because it gave CEOs and IT managers the green light to start cutting their technology budgets, putting their companies in peril. They go on to state that true competitive advantage *can* be found with information systems that support business processes. In chapter 8 we will focus on the use of business processes for competitive advantage.

3. Porter, Michael. "Strategy and the Internet," Harvard Business Review, Vol. 79, No. 3, March 2001. http://hbswk.hbs.edu/item/2165.html

4. Wiseman, C., & MacMillan, I. C. (1984). CREATING COMPETITIVE WEAPONS FROM INFORMATION SYSTEMS. Journal Of Business Strategy, 5(2), 42.

Electronic Data Interchange

One of the ways that information systems have participated in competitive advantage is through integrating the supply chain electronically. This is primarily done through a process called electronic data interchange, or EDI. EDI can be thought of as the *computer-to-computer exchange of business documents in a standard electronic format between business partners.* By integrating suppliers and distributors via EDI, a company can vastly reduce the resources required to manage the relevant information. Instead of manually ordering supplies, the company can simply place an order via the computer and the next time the order process runs, it is ordered.

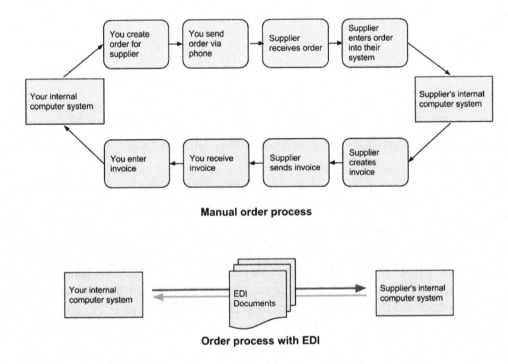

EDI example (click to enlarge)

Collaborative Systems

As organizations began to implement networking technologies, information systems emerged that allowed employees to begin collaborating in different ways. These systems allowed users to brainstorm ideas together without the necessity of physical, face-to-face meetings. Utilizing tools such as discussion boards, document sharing, and video, these systems made it possible for ideas to be shared in new ways and the thought processes behind these ideas to be documented.

Broadly speaking, any software that allows multiple users to interact on a document or topic could be considered collaborative. Electronic mail, a shared Word document, social networks, and discussion boards would fall into this broad definition. However, many software tools have been created that are designed specifically for collaborative purposes. These tools offer a broad spectrum of collaborative functions. Here is just a short list of some collaborative tools available for businesses today:

- Google Drive. Google Drive offers a suite of office applications (such as a word processor, spreadsheet, drawing, presentation) that can be shared between individuals. Multiple users can edit the documents at the same time and threaded comments are available.

- Microsoft SharePoint. SharePoint integrates with Microsoft Office and allows for collaboration using tools most office workers are familiar with. SharePoint was covered in more detail in chapter 5.
- Cisco WebEx. WebEx is a business communications platform that combines video and audio communications and allows participants to interact with each other's computer desktops. WebEx also provides a shared whiteboard and the capability for text-based chat to be going on during the sessions, along with many other features. Mobile editions of WebEx allow for full participation using smartphones and tablets.
- Atlassian Confluence. Confluence provides an all-in-one project-management application that allows users to collaborate on documents and communicate progress. The mobile edition of Confluence allows the project members to stay connected throughout the project.
- IBM Lotus Notes/Domino. One of the first true "groupware" collaboration tools, Lotus Notes (and its web-based cousin, Domino) provides a full suite of collaboration software, including integrated e-mail.

Decision Support Systems

A decision support system (DSS) is an information system built to help an organization make a specific decision or set of decisions. DSSs can exist at different levels of decision-making with the organization, from the CEO to the first-level managers. These systems are designed to take inputs regarding a known (or partially-known) decision-making process and provide the information necessary to make a decision. DSSs generally assist a management-level person in the decision-making process, though some can be designed to automate decision-making.

An organization has a wide variety of decisions to make, ranging from highly structured decisions to unstructured decisions. A structured decision is usually one that is made quite often, and one in which the decision is based directly on the inputs. With structured decisions, once you know the necessary information you also know the decision that needs to be made. For example, inventory reorder levels can be structured decisions: once our inventory of widgets gets below a specific threshold, automatically reorder ten more. Structured decisions are good candidates for automation, but we don't necessarily build decision-support systems for them.

An unstructured decision involves a lot of unknowns. Many times, unstructured decisions are decisions being made for the first time. An information system can support these types of decisions by providing the decision-maker(s) with information-gathering tools and collaborative capabilities. An example of an unstructured decision might be dealing with a labor issue or setting policy for a new technology.

Decision support systems work best when the decision-maker(s) are making semi-structured decisions. A semi-structured decision is one in which most of the factors needed for making the decision are known but human experience and other outside factors may still play a role. A good example of an semi-structured decision would be diagnosing a medical condition (see sidebar).

As with collaborative systems, DSSs can come in many different formats. A nicely designed spreadsheet that allows for input of specific variables and then calculates required outputs could be considered a DSS. Another DSS might be one that assists in determining which products a company should develop. Input into the system could include market research on the product, competitor information, and product development costs. The system would then analyze these inputs based on the specific rules and concepts programmed into it. Finally, the system would report its results, with recommendations and/or key indicators to be used in making a decision. A DSS can be looked at as a tool for competitive advantage in that it can give an organization a mechanism to make wise decisions about products and innovations.

Sidebar: Isabel – A Health Care DSS

A discussed in the text, DSSs are best applied to semi-structured decisions, in which most of the needed inputs are known but human experience and environmental factors also play a role. A good example that is in use today is Isabel, a health care DSS. The creators of Isabel explain how it works:

> Isabel uses the information routinely captured during your workup, whether free text or structured data, and instantaneously provides a diagnosis checklist for review. The checklist contains a list of possible diagnoses with critical "Don't Miss Diagnoses" flagged. When integrated into your EMR system Isabel can provide "one click" seamless diagnosis support with no additional data entry. [5]

Investing in IT for Competitive Advantage

In 2008, Brynjolfsson and McAfee published a study in the *Harvard Business Review* on the role of IT in competitive advantage, entitled "Investing in the IT That Makes a Competitive Difference." Their study confirmed that IT *can* play a role in competitive advantage, if deployed wisely. In their study, they draw three conclusions[6]:

- First, the data show that IT has sharpened differences among companies instead of reducing them. This reflects the fact that while companies have always varied widely in their ability to select, adopt, and exploit innovations, technology has accelerated and amplified these differences.
- Second, good management matters: Highly qualified vendors, consultants, and IT departments might be necessary for the successful implementation of enterprise technologies themselves, but the real value comes from the process innovations that can now be delivered on those platforms. Fostering the right innovations and propagating them widely are both executive responsibilities – ones that can't be delegated.
- Finally, the competitive shakeup brought on by IT is not nearly complete, even in the IT-intensive US economy. We expect to see these altered competitive dynamics in other countries, as well, as their IT investments grow.

5. Taken from http://www.isabelhealthcare.com/home/ourmission. Accessed July 15, 2013.
6. McAfee, Andrew and Brynjolfsson, Erik "Investing in the IT That Makes a Competitive Difference" Harvard Business Review, (July-August, 2008)

Information systems can be used for competitive advantage, but they must be used strategically. Organizations must understand how they want to differentiate themselves and then use all the elements of information systems (hardware, software, data, people, and process) to accomplish that differentiation.

Summary

Information systems are integrated into all components of business today, but can they bring competitive advantage? Over the years, there have been many answers to this question. Early research could not draw any connections between IT and profitability, but later research has shown that the impact can be positive. IT is not a panacea; just purchasing and installing the latest technology will not, by itself, make a company more successful. Instead, the combination of the right technologies and good management, together, will give a company the best chance of a positive result.

Study Questions

1. What is the productivity paradox?

2. Summarize Carr's argument in "Does IT Matter."

3. How is the 2008 study by Brynjolfsson and McAfee different from previous studies? How is it the same?

4. What does it mean for a business to have a competitive advantage?

5. What are the primary activities and support activities of the value chain?

6. What has been the overall impact of the Internet on industry profitability? Who has been the true winner?

7. How does EDI work?

8. Give an example of a semi-structured decision and explain what inputs would be necessary to provide assistance in making the decision.

9. What does a collaborative information system do?

10. How can IT play a role in competitive advantage, according to the 2008 article by Brynjolfsson and McAfee?

Exercises

1. Do some independent research on Nicholas Carr (the author of "IT Doesn't Matter") and explain his current position on the ability of IT to provide competitive advantage.

2. Review the WebEx website. What features of WebEx would contribute to good collaboration? What makes WebEx a better collaboration tool than something like Skype or Google Hangouts?

3. Think of a semi-structured decision that you make in your daily life and build your own DSS using a spreadsheet that would help you make that decision.

Chapter 8: Business Processes

Learning Objectives

Upon successful completion of this chapter, you will be able to:

- define the term *business process*;
- identify the different systems needed to support business processes in an organization;
- explain the value of an enterprise resource planning (ERP) system;
- explain how business process management and business process reengineering work; and
- understand how information technology combined with business processes can bring an organization competitive advantage.

Introduction

The fourth component of information systems is *process*. But what is a process and how does it tie into information systems? And in what ways do processes have a role in business? This chapter will look to answer those questions and also describe how business processes can be used for strategic advantage.

What Is a Business Process?

We have all heard the term *process* before, but what exactly does it mean? A process is a series of tasks that are completed in order to accomplish a goal. A business process, therefore, is a process that is focused on achieving a goal for a business. If you have worked in a business setting, you have participated in a business process. Anything from a simple process for making a sandwich at Subway to building a space shuttle utilizes one or more business processes.

Processes are something that businesses go through every day in order to accomplish their mission. The better their processes, the more effective the business. Some businesses see their processes as a strategy for achieving competitive advantage. A process that achieves its goal in a unique way can set a company apart. A process that eliminates costs can allow a company to lower its prices (or retain more profit).

Documenting a Process

Every day, each of us will conduct many processes without even thinking about them: getting ready for work, using an ATM, reading our e-mail, etc. But as processes grow more complex, they need to be documented. For businesses, it is essential to do this, because it allows them to ensure control over how activities are undertaken in their organization. It also allows for standardization: McDonald's has the same process for building a Big Mac in all of its restaurants.

The simplest way to document a process is to simply create a list. The list shows each step in the process; each step can be checked off upon completion. For example, a simple process, such as how to create an account on eBay, might look like this:

1. Go to ebay.com.

2. Click on "register."

3. Enter your contact information in the "Tell us about you" box.

4. Choose your user ID and password.

5. Agree to User Agreement and Privacy Policy by clicking on "Submit."

For processes that are not so straightforward, documenting the process as a checklist may not be sufficient. For example, here is the process for determining if an article for a term needs to be added to Wikipedia:

1. Search Wikipedia to determine if the term already exists.

2. If the term is found, then an article is already written, so you must think of another term. Go to 1.

3. If the term is not found, then look to see if there is a related term.

4. If there is a related term, then create a redirect.

5. If there is not a related term, then create a new article.

This procedure is relatively simple – in fact, it has the same number of steps as the previous example – but because it has some decision points, it is more difficult to track with as a simple list. In these cases, it may make more sense to use a diagram to document the process:

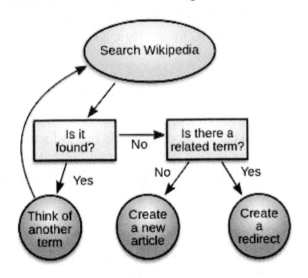

Process diagram for determining if a new term should be added to Wikipedia (click to enlarge). (Public Domain)

Managing Business Process Documentation

As organizations begin to document their processes, it becomes an administrative task to keep track of them. As processes change and improve, it is important to know which processes are the most recent. It is also important to manage the process so that it can be easily updated! The requirement to manage process documentation has been one of the driving forces behind the creation of the *document management system*. A document management system stores and tracks documents and supports the following functions:

- Versions and timestamps. The document management system will keep multiple versions of documents. The most recent version of a document is easy to identify and will be served up by default.

- Approvals and workflows. When a process needs to be changed, the system will manage both access to the documents for editing and the routing of the document for approvals.

- Communication. When a process changes, those who implement the process need to be made aware of the changes. A document management system will notify the appropriate people when a change to a document is approved.

Of course, document management systems are not only used for managing business process documentation. Many other types of documents are managed in these systems, such as legal documents or design documents.

ERP Systems

An enterprise resource planning (ERP) system is a software application with a centralized database that can be used to run an entire company. Let's take a closer look at the definition of each of these components:

- A software application: The system is a software application, which means that it has been developed with specific logic and rules behind it. It has to be installed and configured to work specifically for an individual organization.

- With a centralized database: All data in an ERP system is stored in a single, central database. This centralization is key to the success of an ERP – data entered in one part of the company can be immediately available to other parts of the company.

- That can be used to run an entire company: An ERP can be used to manage an entire organization's operations. If they so wish, companies can purchase modules for an ERP that represent different functions within the organization, such as finance, manufacturing, and sales. Some companies choose to purchase many modules, others choose a subset of the modules.

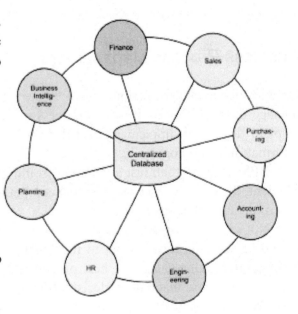

An ERP system (click to enlarge)

An ERP system not only centralizes an organization's data, but the processes it enforces are the processes the organization adopts. When an ERP vendor designs a module, it has to implement the rules for the associated business processes. A selling point of an ERP system is that it has best practices built right into it. In other words, when an organization implements an ERP, it also gets improved best practices as part of the deal!

For many organizations, the implementation of an ERP system is an excellent opportunity to improve their business practices and upgrade their software at the same time. But for others, an ERP brings them a challenge: Is the process embedded in the ERP really better than the process they are currently utilizing?

And if they implement this ERP, and it happens to be the same one that all of their competitors have, will they simply become more like them, making it much more difficult to differentiate themselves?

This has been one of the criticisms of ERP systems: that they commoditize business processes, driving all businesses to use the same processes and thereby lose their uniqueness. The good news is that ERP systems also have the capability to be configured with custom processes. For organizations that want to continue using their own processes or even design new ones, ERP systems offer ways to support this through the use of customizations.

Registered trademark of SAP

But there is a drawback to customizing an ERP system: organizations have to maintain the changes themselves. Whenever an update to the ERP system comes out, any organization that has created a custom process will be required to add that change to their ERP. This will require someone to maintain a listing of these changes and will also require retesting the system every time an upgrade is made. Organizations will have to wrestle with this decision: When should they go ahead and accept the best-practice processes built into the ERP system and when should they spend the resources to develop their own processes? It makes the most sense to only customize those processes that are critical to the competitive advantage of the company.

Some of the best-known ERP vendors are SAP, Microsoft, and Oracle.

Business Process Management

Organizations that are serious about improving their business processes will also create structures to manage those processes. Business process management (BPM) can be thought of as an intentional effort to plan, document, implement, and distribute an organization's business processes with the support of information technology.

BPM is more than just automating some simple steps. While automation can make a business more efficient, it cannot be used to provide a competitive advantage. BPM, on the other hand, can be an integral part of creating that advantage.

Not all of an organization's processes should be managed this way. An organization should look for processes that are essential to the functioning of the business and those that may be used to bring a competitive advantage. The best processes to look at are those that include employees from multiple departments, those that require decision-making that cannot be easily automated, and processes that change based on circumstances.

To make this clear, let's take a look at an example.

Suppose a large clothing retailer is looking to gain a competitive advantage through superior customer service. As part of this, they create a task force to develop a state-of-the-art returns policy that allows customers to return any article of clothing, no questions asked. The organization also decides that, in order to protect the competitive advantage that this returns policy will bring, they will develop their own customization to their ERP system to implement this returns policy. As they prepare to roll out the system, they invest in training for all of their customer-service employees, showing them how to use the new system and specifically how to process returns. Once the updated returns process is implemented, the organization will be able to measure several key indicators about returns that will allow them to adjust the policy as needed. For example, if they find that many women are returning their high-end dresses after wearing them once, they could implement a change to the process that limits – to, say, fourteen days – the time after the original purchase that an item can be returned. As changes to the returns policy are made, the changes are rolled out via internal communications, and updates to the returns processing on the system are made. In our example, the system would no longer allow a dress to be returned after fourteen days without an approved reason.

If done properly, business process management will provide several key benefits to an organization, which can be used to contribute to competitive advantage. These benefits include:

- Empowering employees. When a business process is designed correctly and supported with information technology, employees will be able to implement it on their own authority. In our returns-policy example, an employee would be able to accept returns made before fourteen days or use the system to make determinations on what returns would be allowed after fourteen days.

- Built-in reporting. By building measurement into the programming, the organization can keep up to date on key metrics regarding their processes. In our example, these can be used to improve the returns process and also, ideally, to reduce returns.

- Enforcing best practices. As an organization implements processes supported by information systems, it can work to implement the best practices for that class of business process. In our example, the organization may want to require that all customers returning a product without a receipt show a legal ID. This requirement can be built into the system so that the return will not be processed unless a valid ID number is entered.

- Enforcing consistency. By creating a process and enforcing it with information technology, it is possible to create a consistency across the entire organization. In our example, all stores in the retail chain can enforce the same returns policy. And if the returns policy changes, the change can be instantly enforced across the entire chain.

Business Process Reengineering

As organizations look to manage their processes to gain a competitive advantage, they also need to understand that their existing ways of doing things may not be the most effective or efficient. A process developed in the 1950s is not going to be better just because it is now supported by technology.

In 1990, Michael Hammer published an article in the *Harvard Business Review* entitled "Reengineering Work: Don't Automate, Obliterate." This article put forward the thought that simply automating a bad process does not make it better. Instead, companies should "blow up" their existing processes and develop new processes that take advantage of the new technologies and concepts. He states in the introduction to the article:[1]

Many of our job designs, work flows, control mechanisms, and organizational structures came of age in a different competitive environment and before the advent of the computer. They are geared towards greater efficiency and control. Yet the watchwords of the new decade are innovation and speed, service, and quality.

It is time to stop paving the cow paths. Instead of embedding outdated processes in silicon and software, we should obliterate them and start over. We should "reengineer" our businesses: use the power of modern information technology to radically redesign our business processes in order to achieve dramatic improvements in their performance.

Business process reengineering is not just taking an existing process and automating it. BPR is fully understanding the goals of a process and then dramatically redesigning it from the ground up to achieve

---

1. Hammer, Michael. "Reengineering work: don't automate, obliterate." *Harvard Business Review* 68.4 (1990): 104–112.

dramatic improvements in productivity and quality. But this is easier said than done. Most of us think in terms of how to do small, local improvements to a process; complete redesign requires thinking on a larger scale. Hammer provides some guidelines for how to go about doing business process reengineering:

- Organize around outcomes, not tasks. This simply means to design the process so that, if possible, one person performs all the steps. Instead of repeating one step in the process over and over, the person stays involved in the process from start to finish.

- Have those who use the outcomes of the process perform the process. Using information technology, many simple tasks are now automated, so we can empower the person who needs the outcome of the process to perform it. The example Hammer gives here is purchasing: instead of having every department in the company use a purchasing department to order supplies, have the supplies ordered directly by those who need the supplies using an information system.

- Subsume information-processing work into the real work that produces the information. When one part of the company creates information (like sales information, or payment information), it should be processed by that same department. There is no need for one part of the company to process information created in another part of the company.

- Treat geographically dispersed resources as though they were centralized. With the communications technologies in place today, it becomes easier than ever to not worry about physical location. A multinational organization does not need separate support departments (such as IT, purchasing, etc.) for each location anymore.

- Link parallel activities instead of integrating their results. Departments that work in parallel should be sharing data and communicating with each other during their activities instead of waiting until each group is done and then comparing notes.

- Put the decision points where the work is performed, and build controls into the process. The people who do the work should have decision-making authority and the process itself should have built-in controls using information technology.

- Capture information once, at the source. Requiring information to be entered more than once causes delays and errors. With information technology, an organization can capture it once and then make it available whenever needed.

These principles may seem like common sense today, but in 1990 they took the business world by storm. Hammer gives example after example of how organizations improved their business processes by many orders of magnitude without adding any new employees, simply by changing how they did things (see sidebar).

Unfortunately, business process reengineering got a bad name in many organizations. This was because it was used as an excuse for cost cutting that really had nothing to do with BPR. For example, many companies simply used it as an excuse for laying off part of their workforce. Today, however, many of the principles of BPR have been integrated into businesses and are considered part of good business-process management.

Sidebar: Reengineering the College Bookstore

The process of purchasing the correct textbooks in a timely manner for college classes has always been problematic. And now, with online bookstores such as Amazon competing directly with the college bookstore for students' purchases, the college bookstore is under pressure to justify its existence.

But college bookstores have one big advantage over their competitors: they have access to students' data. In other words, once a student has registered for classes, the bookstore knows exactly what books that student will need for the upcoming term. To leverage this advantage and take advantage of new technologies, the bookstore wants to implement a new process that will make purchasing books through the bookstore advantageous to students. Though they may not be able to compete on price, they can provide other advantages, such as reducing the time it takes to find the books and the ability to guarantee that the book is the correct one for the class. In order to do this, the bookstore will need to undertake a process redesign.

The goal of the process redesign is simple: capture a higher percentage of students as customers of the bookstore. After diagramming the existing process and meeting with student focus groups, the bookstore comes up with a new process. In the new process, the bookstore utilizes information technology to reduce the amount of work the students need to do in order to get their books. In this new process, the bookstore sends the students an e-mail with a list of all the books required for their upcoming classes. By clicking a link in this e-mail, the students can log into the bookstore, confirm their books, and purchase the books. The bookstore will then deliver the books to the students.

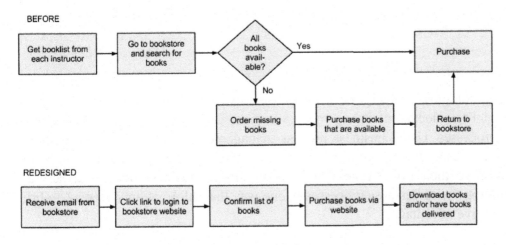

College bookstore process redesign (click to enlarge)

ISO Certification

Many organizations now claim that they are using best practices when it comes to business processes. In order to set themselves apart and prove to their customers (and potential customers) that they are indeed doing this, these organizations are seeking out an ISO 9000 certification. ISO is an acronym for International Standards Organization (website here). This body defines quality standards that organizations can implement to show that they are, indeed, managing business processes in an effective way. The ISO 9000 certification is focused on quality management.

In order to receive ISO certification, an organization must be audited and found to meet specific criteria. In its most simple form, the auditors perform the following review:

- Tell me what you do *(describe the business process)*.
- Show me where it says that *(reference the process documentation)*.
- Prove that this is what happened *(exhibit evidence in documented records)*.

Over the years, this certification has evolved and many branches of the certification now exist. ISO certification is one way to separate an organization from others. You can find out more about the ISO 9000 standard here.

Summary

The advent of information technologies has had a huge impact on how organizations design, implement, and support business processes. From document management systems to ERP systems, information systems are tied into organizational processes. Using business process management, organizations can empower employees and leverage their processes for competitive advantage. Using business process reengineering, organizations can vastly improve their effectiveness and the quality of their products and services. Integrating information technology with business processes is one way that information systems can bring an organization lasting competitive advantage.

Study Questions

1. What does the term *business process* mean?
2. What are three examples of business process from a job you have had or an organization you have observed?
3. What is the value in documenting a business process?
4. What is an ERP system? How does an ERP system enforce best practices for an organization?
5. What is one of the criticisms of ERP systems?

6. What is business process reengineering? How is it different from incrementally improving a process?

7. Why did BPR get a bad name?

8. List the guidelines for redesigning a business process.

9. What is business process management? What role does it play in allowing a company to differentiate itself?

10. What does ISO certification signify?

Exercises

1. Think of a business process that you have had to perform in the past. How would you document this process? Would a diagram make more sense than a checklist? Document the process both as a checklist and as a diagram.

2. Review the return policies at your favorite retailer, then answer this question: What information systems do you think would need to be in place to support their return policy.

3. If you were implementing an ERP system, in which cases would you be more inclined to modify the ERP to match your business processes? What are the drawbacks of doing this?

4. Which ERP is the best? Do some original research and compare three leading ERP systems to each other. Write a two- to three-page paper that compares their features.

Chapter 9: The People in Information Systems

Learning Objectives

Upon successful completion of this chapter, you will be able to:

- describe each of the different roles that people play in the design, development, and use of information systems;
- understand the different career paths available to those who work with information systems;
- explain the importance of where the information-systems function is placed in an organization; and
- describe the different types of users of information systems.

Introduction

In the opening chapters of this text, we focused on the technology behind information systems: hardware, software, data, and networking. In the last chapter, we discussed business processes and the key role they can play in the success of a business. In this chapter, we will be discussing the last component of an information system: people.

People are involved in information systems in just about every way you can think of: people imagine information systems, people develop information systems, people support information systems, and, perhaps most importantly, people *use* information systems.

The Creators of Information Systems

The first group of people we are going to look at play a role in designing, developing, and building information systems. These people are generally very technical and have a background in programming and mathematics. Just about everyone who works in the creation of information systems has a minimum of a bachelor's degree in computer science or information systems, though that is not necessarily a requirement. We will be looking at the process of creating information systems in more detail in chapter 10.

Systems Analyst

The role of the systems analyst is to straddle the divide between identifying business needs and imagining a new or redesigned computer-based system to fulfill those needs. This individual will work with a person, team, or department with business requirements and identify the specific details of a system that needs to be built. Generally, this will require the analyst to have a good understanding of the business itself , the business processes involved, and the ability to document them well. The analyst will identify the different stakeholders in the system and work to involve the appropriate individuals in the process.

Once the requirements are determined, the analyst will begin the process of translating these requirements into an information-systems design. A good analyst will understand what different technological solutions will work and provide several different alternatives to the requester, based on the company's budgetary constraints, technology constraints, and culture. Once the solution is selected, the analyst will create a detailed document describing the new system. This new document will require that the analyst understand how to speak in the technical language of systems developers.

A systems analyst generally is not the one who does the actual development of the information system. The design document created by the systems analyst provides the detail needed to create the system and is handed off to a programmer (or team of programmers) to do the actual creation of the system. In some cases, however, a systems analyst may go ahead and create the system that he or she designed. This person is sometimes referred to as a programmer-analyst.

In other cases, the system may be assembled from off-the-shelf components by a person called a systems integrator. This is a specific type of systems analyst that understands how to get different software packages to work with each other.

To become a systems analyst, you should have a background both in the business and in systems design. Many analysts first worked as programmers and/or had experience in the business before becoming systems analysts.

Programmer

Programmers spend their time writing computer code in a programming language. In the case of systems development, programmers generally attempt to fulfill the design specifications given to them by a systems analyst. Many different styles of programming exist: a programmer may work alone for long stretches of time or may work in a team with other programmers. A programmer needs to be able to understand complex processes and also the intricacies of one or more programming languages. Generally, a programmer is very proficient in mathematics, as mathematical concepts underlie most programming code.

Computer Engineer

Computer engineers design the computing devices that we use every day. There are many types of computer engineers, who work on a variety of different types of devices and systems. Some of the more prominent engineering jobs are as follows:

- Hardware engineer. A hardware engineer designs hardware components, such as microprocessors. Many times, a hardware engineer is at the cutting edge of computing technology, creating something brand new. Other times, the hardware engineer's job is to engineer an existing component to work faster or use less power. Many times, a hardware engineer's job is to write code to create a program that will be implemented directly on a computer chip.

- Software engineer. Software engineers do not actually design devices; instead, they create new programming languages and operating systems, working at the lowest levels of the hardware to develop new kinds of software to run on the hardware.

- Systems engineer. A systems engineer takes the components designed by other engineers and makes them all work together. For example, to build a computer, the mother board, processor, memory, and hard disk all have to work together. A systems engineer has experience with many different types of hardware and software and knows how to integrate them to create new functionality.
- Network engineer. A network engineer's job is to understand the networking requirements of an organization and then design a communications system to meet those needs, using the networking hardware and software available.

There are many different types of computer engineers, and often the job descriptions overlap. While many may call themselves engineers based on a company job title, there is also a professional designation of "professional engineer," which has specific requirements behind it. In the US, each state has its own set of requirements for the use of this title, as do different countries around the world. Most often, it involves a professional licensing exam.

Information-Systems Operations and Administration

Another group of information-systems professionals are involved in the day-to-day operations and administration of IT. These people must keep the systems running and up-to-date so that the rest of the organization can make the most effective use of these resources.

Computer Operator

A computer operator is the person who keeps the large computers running. This person's job is to oversee the mainframe computers and data centers in organizations. Some of their duties include keeping the operating systems up to date, ensuring available memory and disk storage, and overseeing the physical environment of the computer. Since mainframe computers increasingly have been replaced with servers, storage management systems, and other platforms, computer operators' jobs have grown broader and include working with these specialized systems.

Database Administrator

A database administrator (DBA) is the person who manages the databases for an organization. This person creates and maintains databases that are used as part of applications or the data warehouse. The DBA also consults with systems analysts and programmers on projects that require access to or the creation of databases.

Help-Desk/Support Analyst

Most mid-size to large organizations have their own information-technology help desk. The help desk is the first line of support for computer users in the company. Computer users who are having problems or need information can contact the help desk for assistance. Many times, a help-desk worker is a junior-level employee who does not necessarily know how to answer all of the questions that come his or her way. In these cases, help-desk analysts work with senior-level support analysts or have a computer knowledgebase at their disposal to help them investigate the problem at hand. The help desk is a great place to break into working in IT because it exposes you to all of the different technologies within the company. A successful help-desk analyst should have good people and communications skills, as well as at least junior-level IT skills.

Trainer

A computer trainer conducts classes to teach people specific computer skills. For example, if a new ERP system is being installed in an organization, one part of the implementation process is to teach all of the users how to use the new system. A trainer may work for a software company and be contracted to come in to conduct classes when needed; a trainer may work for a company that offers regular training sessions; or a trainer may be employed full time for an organization to handle all of their computer instruction needs. To be successful as a trainer, you need to be able to communicate technical concepts well and also have a lot of patience!

Managing Information Systems

The management of information-systems functions is critical to the success of information systems within the organization. Here are some of the jobs associated with the management of information systems.

CIO

The CIO, or chief information officer, is the head of the information-systems function. This person aligns the plans and operations of the information systems with the strategic goals of the organization. This includes tasks such as budgeting, strategic planning, and personnel decisions for the information-systems function. The CIO must also be the face of the IT department within the organization. This involves working with senior leaders in all parts of the organization to ensure good communication and planning.

Interestingly, the CIO position does not necessarily require a lot of technical expertise. While helpful, it is more important for this person to have good management skills and understand the business. Many organizations do not have someone with the title of CIO; instead, the head of the information-systems function is called vice president of information systems or director of information systems.

Functional Manager

As an information-systems organization becomes larger, many of the different functions are grouped together and led by a manager. These functional managers report to the CIO and manage the employees specific to their function. For example, in a large organization, there is a group of systems analysts who report to a manager of the systems-analysis function. For more insight into how this might look, see the discussion later in the chapter of how information systems are organized.

ERP Management

Organizations using an ERP require one or more individuals to manage these systems. These people make sure that the ERP system is completely up to date, work to implement any changes to the ERP that are needed, and consult with various user departments on needed reports or data extracts.

Project Managers

Information-systems projects are notorious for going over budget and being delivered late. In many cases, a failed IT project can spell doom for a company. A project manager is responsible for keeping projects on time and on budget. This person works with the stakeholders of the project to keep the team organized and communicates the status of the project to management. A project manager does not have authority over the project team; instead, the project manager coordinates schedules and resources in order to maximize the project outcomes. A project manager must be a good communicator and an extremely organized person. A project manager should also have good people skills. Many organizations require each of their project managers to become certified as a project management professional (PMP).

Information-Security Officer

An information-security officer is in charge of setting information-security policies for an organization, and then overseeing the implementation of those policies. This person may have one or more people reporting to them as part of the information-security team. As information has become a critical asset, this position has become highly valued. The information-security officer must ensure that the organization's information remains secure from both internal and external threats.

Emerging Roles

As technology evolves, many new roles are becoming more common as other roles fade. For example, as we enter the age of "big data," we are seeing the need for more data analysts and business-intelligence specialists. Many companies are now hiring social-media experts and mobile-technology specialists. The increased use of cloud computing and virtual-machine technologies also is breeding demand for expertise in those areas.

Career Paths in Information Systems

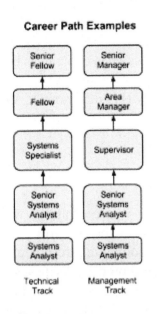

Career Path Examples

Technical Track / Management Track

These job descriptions do not represent all possible jobs within an information-systems organization. Larger organizations will have more specialized roles; smaller organizations may combine some of these roles. Many of these roles may exist outside of a traditional information-systems organization, as we will discuss below.

Working with information systems can be a rewarding career choice. Whether you want to be involved in very technical jobs (programmer, database administrator), or you want to be involved in working with people (systems analyst, trainer), there are many different career paths available.

Many times, those in technical jobs who want career advancement find themselves in a dilemma: do they want to continue doing technical work, where sometimes their advancement options are limited, or do they want to become a manager of other employees and put themselves on a management career track? In many cases, those proficient in technical skills are not gifted with managerial skills. Some organizations, especially those that highly value their technically skilled employees, will create a technical track that exists in parallel to the management track so that they can retain employees who are contributing to the organization with their technical skills.

Sidebar: Are Certifications Worth Pursuing?

As technology is becoming more and more important to businesses, hiring employees with technical skills is becoming critical. But how can an organization ensure that the person they are hiring has the necessary skills? These days, many organizations are including technical certifications as a prerequisite for getting hired.

Certifications are designations given by a certifying body that someone has a specific level of knowledge in a specific technology. This certifying body is often the vendor of the product itself, though independent certifying organizations, such as CompTIA, also exist. Many of these organizations offer certification tracks, allowing a beginning certificate as a prerequisite to getting more advanced certificates. To get a certificate, you generally attend one or more training classes and then take one or more certification exams. Passing the exams with a certain score will qualify you for a certificate. In most cases, these classes and certificates are not free and, in fact, can run into the thousands of dollars. Some examples of the certifications in highest demand include Microsoft (software certifications), Cisco (networking), and SANS (security).

For many working in IT (or thinking about an IT career), determining whether to pursue one or more of these certifications is an important question. For many jobs, such as those involving networking or security, a certificate will be required by the employer as a way to determine which potential employees have a basic level of skill. For those who are already in an IT career, a more advanced certificate may lead to a promotion. There are other cases, however, when experience with a certain technology will negate the need for certification. For those wondering about the importance of certification, the best solution is to talk to potential employers and those already working in the field to determine the best choice.

Organizing the Information-Systems Function

In the early years of computing, the information-systems function (generally called data processing) was placed in the finance or accounting department of the organization. As computing became more important, a separate information-systems function was formed, but it still was generally placed under the CFO and considered to be an administrative function of the company. In the 1980s and 1990s, when companies began networking internally and then linking up to the Internet, the information-systems function was combined with the telecommunications functions and designated the information technology (IT) department. As the role of information technology continued to increase, its place in the organization also moved up the ladder. In many organizations today, the head of IT (the CIO) reports directly to the CEO.

Where in the Organization Should IS Be?

Before the advent of the personal computer, the information-systems function was centralized within organizations in order to maximize control over computing resources. When the PC began proliferating, many departments within organizations saw it as a chance to gain some computing resources for themselves. Some departments created an internal information-systems group, complete with systems analysts, programmers, and even database administrators. These departmental-IS groups were dedicated to the information needs of their own departments, providing quicker turnaround and higher levels of service than a centralized IT department. However, having several IS groups within an organization led to a lot of inefficiencies: there were now several people performing the same jobs in different departments. This decentralization also led to company data being stored in several places all over the company. In some organizations, a "matrix" reporting structure has developed, in which IT personnel are placed within a department and report to both the department management and the functional management within IS. The advantages of dedicated IS personnel for each department are weighed against the need for more control over the strategic information resources of the company.

For many companies, these questions are resolved by the implementation of the ERP system (see discussion of ERP in chapter 8). Because an ERP system consolidates most corporate data back into a single database, the implementation of an ERP system requires organizations to find "islands" of data so that they can integrate them back into the corporate system. The ERP allows organizations to regain control of their information and influences organizational decisions throughout the company.

Outsourcing

Many times, an organization needs a specific skill for a limited period of time. Instead of training an existing employee or hiring someone new, it may make more sense to outsource the job. Outsourcing can be used in many different situations within the information-systems function, such as the design and creation of a new website or the upgrade of an ERP system. Some organizations see outsourcing as a cost-cutting move, contracting out a whole group or department.

New Models of Organizations

The integration of information technology has influenced the structure of organizations. The increased ability to communicate and share information has led to a "flattening" of the organizational structure due to the removal of one or more layers of management.

Another organizational change enabled by information systems is the network-based organizational structure. In a networked-based organizational structure, groups of employees can work somewhat independently to accomplish a project. In a networked organization, people with the right skills are brought together for a project and then released to work on other projects when that project is over. These groups are somewhat informal and allow for all members of the group to maximize their effectiveness.

Information-Systems Users – Types of Users

Besides the people who work to create, administer, and manage information systems, there is one more extremely important group of people: the users of information systems. This group represents a very large percentage of the people involved. If the user is not able to successfully learn and use an information system, the system is doomed to failure.

One tool that can be used to understand how users will adopt a new technology comes from a 1962 study by Everett Rogers. In his book, *Diffusion of Innovation,*[1] Rogers studied how farmers adopted new technologies, and he noticed that the adoption rate started slowly and then dramatically increased once adoption hit a certain point. He identified five specific types of technology adopters:

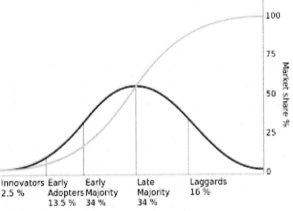

Technology adoption user types (click to enlarge). *(Public Domain)*

- Innovators. Innovators are the first individuals to adopt a new technology. Innovators are willing to take risks, are the youngest in age, have the highest social class, have great financial liquidity, are very social, and have the closest contact with scientific sources and interaction with other innovators. Risk tolerance has them adopting technologies that may ultimately fail. Financial resources help absorb these failures (Rogers 1962 5th ed, p. 282).

- Early adopters. The early adopters are those who adopt innovation after a technology has been introduced and proven. These individuals have the highest degree of opinion leadership among the other adopter categories, which means that they can influence the opinions of the largest majority. They are typically younger in age, have higher social status, more financial liquidity, more advanced education, and are more socially aware than later adopters. These people are more discrete in adoption choices than innovators, and realize judicious choice of adoption will help them maintain a central communication position (Rogers 1962 5th ed, p. 283).

- Early majority. Individuals in this category adopt an innovation after a varying degree of time. This time of adoption is significantly longer than the innovators and early adopters. This group tends to be slower in the adoption process, has above average social status, has contact with early

1. Rogers, E. M. (1962). Diffusion of innovations. New York: Free Press

adopters, and seldom holds positions of opinion leadership in a system (Rogers 1962 5th ed, p. 283).

- Late majority. The late majority will adopt an innovation after the average member of the society. These individuals approach an innovation with a high degree of skepticism, have below average social status, very little financial liquidity, are in contact with others in the late majority and the early majority, and show very little opinion leadership.

- Laggards. Individuals in this category are the last to adopt an innovation. Unlike those in the previous categories, individuals in this category show no opinion leadership. These individuals typically have an aversion to change-agents and tend to be advanced in age. Laggards typically tend to be focused on "traditions," are likely to have the lowest social status and the lowest financial liquidity, be oldest of all other adopters, and be in contact with only family and close friends.

These five types of users can be translated into information-technology adopters as well, and provide additional insight into how to implement new information systems within an organization. For example, when rolling out a new system, IT may want to identify the innovators and early adopters within the organization and work with them first, then leverage their adoption to drive the rest of the implementation.

Summary

In this chapter, we have reviewed the many different categories of individuals who make up the people component of information systems. The world of information technology is changing so fast that new roles are being created all the time, and roles that existed for decades are being phased out. That said, this chapter should have given you a good idea of the importance of the people component of information systems.

Study Questions

1. Describe the role of a systems analyst.
2. What are some of the different roles for a computer engineer?
3. What are the duties of a computer operator?
4. What does the CIO do?
5. Describe the job of a project manager.
6. Explain the point of having two different career paths in information systems.
7. What are the advantages and disadvantages of centralizing the IT function?
8. What impact has information technology had on the way companies are organized?
9. What are the five types of information-systems users?
10. Why would an organization outsource?

Exercises

1. Which IT job would you like to have? Do some original research and write a two-page paper describing the duties of the job you are interested in.

2. Spend a few minutes on Dice or Monster to find IT jobs in your area. What IT jobs are currently available? Write up a two-page paper describing three jobs, their starting salary (if listed), and the skills and education needed for the job.

3. How is the IT function organized in your school or place of employment? Create an organization chart showing how the IT organization fits into your overall organization. Comment on how centralized or decentralized the IT function is.

4. What type of IT user are you? Take a look at the five types of technology adopters and then write a one-page summary of where you think you fit in this model.

Chapter 10: Information Systems Development

Learning Objectives

Upon successful completion of this chapter, you will be able to:

- explain the overall process of developing a new software application;
- explain the differences between software development methodologies;
- understand the different types of programming languages used to develop software;
- understand some of the issues surrounding the development of websites and mobile applications; and
- identify the four primary implementation policies.

Introduction

When someone has an idea for a new function to be performed by a computer, how does that idea become reality? If a company wants to implement a new business process and needs new hardware or software to support it, how do they go about making it happen? In this chapter, we will discuss the different methods of taking those ideas and bringing them to reality, a process known as information systems development.

Programming

As we learned in chapter 2, software is created via programming. Programming is the process of creating a set of logical instructions for a digital device to follow using a programming language. The process of programming is sometimes called "coding" because the syntax of a programming language is not in a form that everyone can understand – it is in "code."

The process of developing good software is usually not as simple as sitting down and writing some code. True, sometimes a programmer can quickly write a short program to solve a need. But most of the time, the creation of software is a resource-intensive process that involves several different groups of people in an organization. In the following sections, we are going to review several different methodologies for software development.

Systems-Development Life Cycle

The first development methodology we are going to review is the systems-development life cycle (SDLC). This methodology was first developed in the 1960s to manage the large software projects associated with corporate systems running on mainframes. It is a very structured and risk-averse methodology designed to manage large projects that included multiple programmers and systems that would have a large impact on the organization.

Various definitions of the SDLC methodology exist, but most contain the following phases.

1. Preliminary Analysis. In this phase, a review is done of the request. Is creating a solution possible? What alternatives exist? What is currently being done about it? Is this project a good fit for our organization? A key part of this step is a feasibility analysis, which includes an analysis of the technical feasibility (is it possible to create this?), the economic feasibility (can we afford to do this?), and the legal feasibility (are we allowed to do this?). This step is important in determining if the project should even get started.

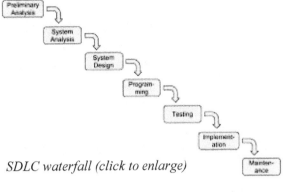

SDLC waterfall (click to enlarge)

2. System Analysis. In this phase, one or more system analysts work with different stakeholder groups to determine the specific requirements for the new system. No programming is done in this step. Instead, procedures are documented, key players are interviewed, and data requirements are developed in order to get an overall picture of exactly what the system is supposed to do. The result of this phase is a system-requirements document.

3. System Design. In this phase, a designer takes the system-requirements document created in the previous phase and develops the specific technical details required for the system. It is in this phase that the business requirements are translated into specific technical requirements. The design for the user interface, database, data inputs and outputs, and reporting are developed here. The result of this phase is a system-design document. This document will have everything a programmer will need to actually create the system.

4. Programming. The code finally gets written in the programming phase. Using the system-design document as a guide, a programmer (or team of programmers) develop the program. The result of this phase is an initial working program that meets the requirements laid out in the system-analysis phase and the design developed in the system-design phase.

5. Testing. In the testing phase, the software program developed in the previous phase is put through a series of structured tests. The first is a unit test, which tests individual parts of the code for errors or bugs. Next is a system test, where the different components of the system are tested to ensure that they work together properly. Finally, the user-acceptance test allows those that will be using the software to test the system to ensure that it meets their standards. Any bugs, errors, or problems found during testing are addressed and then tested again.

6. Implementation. Once the new system is developed and tested, it has to be implemented in the organization. This phase includes training the users, providing documentation, and conversion from any previous system to the new system. Implementation can take many forms, depending on the type of system, the number and type of users, and how urgent it is that the system become operational. These different forms of implementation are covered later in the chapter.

7. Maintenance. This final phase takes place once the implementation phase is complete. In this phase, the system has a structured support process in place: reported bugs are fixed and requests for new features are evaluated and implemented; system updates and backups are performed on a regular basis.

The SDLC methodology is sometimes referred to as the waterfall methodology to represent how each step is a separate part of the process; only when one step is completed can another step begin. After each step, an organization must decide whether to move to the next step or not. This methodology has been criticized for being quite rigid. For example, changes to the requirements are not allowed once the process has begun. No software is available until after the programming phase.

Again, SDLC was developed for large, structured projects. Projects using SDLC can sometimes take months or years to complete. Because of its inflexibility and the availability of new programming techniques and tools, many other software-development methodologies have been developed. Many of these retain some of the underlying concepts of SDLC but are not as rigid.

Rapid Application Development

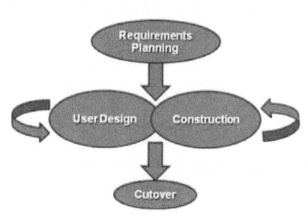

The RAD methodology (Public Domain)

Rapid application development (RAD) is a software-development (or systems-development) methodology that focuses on quickly building a working model of the software, getting feedback from users, and then using that feedback to update the working model. After several iterations of development, a final version is developed and implemented.

The RAD methodology consists of four phases:

1. Requirements Planning. This phase is similar to the preliminary-analysis, system-analysis, and design phases of the SDLC. In this phase, the overall requirements for the system are defined, a team is identified, and feasibility is determined.

2. User Design. In this phase, representatives of the users work with the system analysts, designers, and programmers to interactively create the design of the system. One technique for working with all of these various stakeholders is the so-called JAD session. JAD is an acronym for joint application development. A JAD session gets all of the stakeholders together to have a

structured discussion about the design of the system. Application developers also sit in on this meeting and observe, trying to understand the essence of the requirements.

3. Construction. In the construction phase, the application developers, working with the users, build the next version of the system. This is an interactive process, and changes can be made as developers are working on the program. This step is executed in parallel with the User Design step in an iterative fashion, until an acceptable version of the product is developed.

4. Cutover. In this step, which is similar to the implementation step of the SDLC, the system goes live. All steps required to move from the previous state to the use of the new system are completed here.

As you can see, the RAD methodology is much more compressed than SDLC. Many of the SDLC steps are combined and the focus is on user participation and iteration. This methodology is much better suited for smaller projects than SDLC and has the added advantage of giving users the ability to provide feedback throughout the process. SDLC requires more documentation and attention to detail and is well suited to large, resource-intensive projects. RAD makes more sense for smaller projects that are less resource-intensive and need to be developed quickly.

Agile Methodologies

Agile methodologies are a group of methodologies that utilize incremental changes with a focus on quality and attention to detail. Each increment is released in a specified period of time (called a time box), creating a regular release schedule with very specific objectives. While considered a separate methodology from RAD, they share some of the same principles: iterative development, user interaction, ability to change. The agile methodologies are based on the "Agile Manifesto," first released in 2001.

The characteristics of agile methods include:

- small cross-functional teams that include development-team members and users;
- daily status meetings to discuss the current state of the project;
- short time-frame increments (from days to one or two weeks) for each change to be completed; and
- at the end of each iteration, a working project is completed to demonstrate to the stakeholders.

The goal of the agile methodologies is to provide the flexibility of an iterative approach while ensuring a quality product.

Lean Methodology

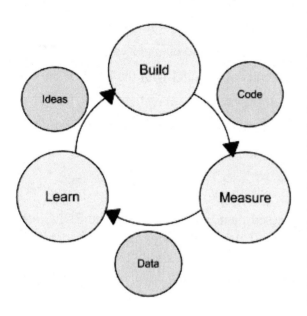

The lean methodology (click to enlarge)

One last methodology we will discuss is a relatively new concept taken from the business bestseller *The Lean Startup,* by Eric Reis. In this methodology, the focus is on taking an initial idea and developing a minimum viable product (MVP). The MVP is a working software application with just enough functionality to demonstrate the idea behind the project. Once the MVP is developed, it is given to potential users for review. Feedback on the MVP is generated in two forms: (1) direct observation and discussion with the users, and (2) usage statistics gathered from the software itself. Using these two forms of feedback, the team determines whether they should continue in the same direction or rethink the core idea behind the project, change the functions, and create a new MVP. This change in strategy is called a pivot. Several iterations of the MVP are developed, with new functions added each time based on the feedback, until a final product is completed.

The biggest difference between the lean methodology and the other methodologies is that the full set of requirements for the system are not known when the project is launched. As each iteration of the project is released, the statistics and feedback gathered are used to determine the requirements. The lean methodology works best in an entrepreneurial environment where a company is interested in determining if their idea for a software application is worth developing.

Sidebar: The Quality Triangle

When developing software, or any sort of product or service, there exists a tension between the developers and the different stakeholder groups, such as management, users, and investors. This tension relates to how quickly the software can be developed (time), how much money will be spent (cost), and how well it will be built (quality). The quality triangle is a simple concept. It states that for any product or service being developed, you can only address two of the following: time, cost, and quality.

So what does it mean that you can only address two of the three? It means that you cannot complete a low-cost, high-quality project in a small amount of time. However, if you are willing or able to spend a lot of money, then a project can be completed quickly with high-quality results (through hiring more good programmers). If a project's completion date is not a priority, then it can be completed at a lower cost with higher-quality results. Of

The quality triangle

course, these are just generalizations, and different projects may not fit this model perfectly. But overall, this model helps us understand the tradeoffs that we must make when we are developing new products and services.

Programming Languages

As I noted earlier, software developers create software using one of several programming languages. A programming language is an artificial language that provides a way for a programmer to create structured code to communicate logic in a format that can be executed by the computer hardware. Over the past few decades, many different types of programming languages have evolved to meet many different needs. One way to characterize programming languages is by their "generation."

Generations of Programming Languages

Early languages were specific to the type of hardware that had to be programmed; each type of computer hardware had a different low-level programming language (in fact, even today there are differences at the lower level, though they are now obscured by higher-level programming languages). In these early languages, very specific instructions had to be entered line by line – a tedious process.

First-generation languages are called machine code. In machine code, programming is done by directly setting actual ones and zeroes (the bits) in the program using binary code. Here is an example program that adds 1234 and 4321 using machine language:

```
10111001 00000000
11010010 10100001
00000100 00000000
10001001 00000000
00001110 10001011
00000000 00011110
00000000 00011110
00000000 00000010
10111001 00000000
11100001 00000011
00010000 11000011
10001001 10100011
00001110 00000100
00000010 00000000
```

Assembly language is the second-generation language. Assembly language gives english-like phrases to the machine-code instructions, making it easier to program. An assembly-language program must be run through an assembler, which converts it into machine code. Here is an example program that adds 1234 and 4321 using assembly language:

```
MOV CX,1234
MOV DS:[0],CX
MOV CX,4321
MOV AX,DS:[0]
MOV BX,DS:[2]
ADD AX,BX
MOV DS:[4],AX
```

Third-generation languages are not specific to the type of hardware on which they run and are much more like spoken languages. Most third-generation languages must be compiled, a process that converts them into machine code. Well-known third-generation languages include BASIC, C, Pascal, and Java. Here is an example using BASIC:

```
A=1234
B=4321
C=A+B
END
```

Fourth-generation languages are a class of programming tools that enable fast application development using intuitive interfaces and environments. Many times, a fourth-generation language has a very specific purpose, such as database interaction or report-writing. These tools can be used by those with very little formal training in programming and allow for the quick development of applications and/or functionality. Examples of fourth-generation languages include: Clipper, FOCUS, FoxPro, SQL, and SPSS.

Why would anyone want to program in a lower-level language when they require so much more work? The answer is similar to why some prefer to drive stick-shift automobiles instead of automatic transmission: control and efficiency. Lower-level languages, such as assembly language, are much more efficient and execute much more quickly. You have finer control over the hardware as well. Sometimes, a combination of higher- and lower-level languages are mixed together to get the best of both worlds: the programmer will create the overall structure and interface using a higher-level language but will use lower-level languages for the parts of the program that are used many times or require more precision.

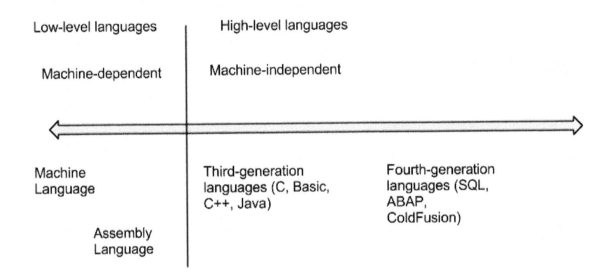

The programming language spectrum (click to enlarge)

Compiled vs. Interpreted

Besides classifying a program language based on its generation, it can also be classified by whether it is compiled or interpreted. As we have learned, a computer language is written in a human-readable form. In a compiled language, the program code is translated into a machine-readable form called an executable that can be run on the hardware. Some well-known compiled languages include C, C++, and COBOL.

An interpreted language is one that requires a runtime program to be installed in order to execute. This runtime program then interprets the program code line by line and runs it. Interpreted languages are generally easier to work with but also are slower and require more system resources. Examples of popular interpreted languages include BASIC, PHP, PERL, and Python. The web languages of HTML and Javascript would also be considered interpreted because they require a browser in order to run.

The Java programming language is an interesting exception to this classification, as it is actually a hybrid of the two. A program written in Java is partially compiled to create a program that can be understood by the Java Virtual Machine (JVM). Each type of operating system has its own JVM which must be installed, which is what allows Java programs to run on many different types of operating systems.

Procedural vs. Object-Oriented

A procedural programming language is designed to allow a programmer to define a specific starting point for the program and then execute sequentially. All early programming languages worked this way. As user interfaces became more interactive and graphical, it made sense for programming languages to evolve to allow the user to define the flow of the program. The object-oriented programming language is set up so that the programmer defines "objects" that can take certain actions based on input from the user. In other words, a procedural program focuses on the sequence of activities to be performed; an object-oriented program focuses on the different items being manipulated.

For example, in a human-resources system, an "EMPLOYEE" object would be needed. If the program needed to retrieve or set data regarding an employee, it would first create an employee object in the program and then set or retrieve the values needed. Every object has properties, which are descriptive fields associated with the object. In the example below, an employee object has the properties "Name", "Employee number", "Birthdate" and "Date of hire". An object also has "methods", which can take actions related to the object. In the example, there are two methods. The first is "ComputePay()", which will return the current amount owed the employee. The second is "ListEmployees()", which will retrieve a list of employees who report to this employee.

Object: EMPLOYEE
Name
Employee number
Birthdate
Date of hire
ComputePay()
ListEmployees()

Figure: An example of an object

Sidebar: What is COBOL?

If you have been around business programming very long, you may have heard about the COBOL programming language. COBOL is a procedural, compiled language that at one time was the primary programming language for business applications. Invented in 1959 for use on large mainframe computers, COBOL is an abbreviation of common business-oriented language. With the advent of more efficient programming languages, COBOL is now rarely seen outside of old, legacy applications.

Programming Tools

To write a program, a programmer needs little more than a text editor and a good idea. However, to be productive, he or she must be able to check the syntax of the code, and, in some cases, compile the code. To be more efficient at programming, additional tools, such as an integrated development environment (IDE) or computer-aided software-engineering (CASE) tools, can be used.

Integrated Development Environment

For most programming languages, an IDE can be used. An IDE provides a variety of tools for the programmer, and usually includes:

- an editor for writing the program that will color-code or highlight keywords from the programming language;
- a help system that gives detailed documentation regarding the programming language;
- a compiler/interpreter, which will allow the programmer to run the program;
- a debugging tool, which will provide the programmer details about the execution of the program in order to resolve problems in the code; and

- a check-in/check-out mechanism, which allows for a team of programmers to work together on a project and not write over each other's code changes.

Probably the most popular IDE software package right now is Microsoft's Visual Studio. Visual Studio is the IDE for all of Microsoft's programming languages, including Visual Basic, Visual C++, and Visual C#.

CASE Tools

While an IDE provides several tools to assist the programmer in writing the program, the code still must be written. Computer-aided software-engineering (CASE) tools allow a designer to develop software with little or no programming. Instead, the CASE tool writes the code for the designer. CASE tools come in many varieties, but their goal is to generate quality code based on input created by the designer.

Sidebar: Building a Website

In the early days of the World Wide Web, the creation of a website required knowing how to use hypertext markup language (HTML). Today, most websites are built with a variety of tools, but the final product that is transmitted to a browser is still HTML. HTML, at its simplest, is a text language that allows you to define the different components of a web page. These definitions are handled through the use of HTML tags, which consist of text between brackets. For example, an HTML tag can tell the browser to show a word in italics, to link to another web page, or to insert an image. In the example below, some text is being defined as a heading while other text is being emphasized.

```
<h1>This is a first-level heading</h1>
Here is some text. <em>Here is some emphasized text.</em>
<h2>Here is a second-level heading</h2>
Here is some more text.
```

Simple HTML

This is a first-level heading

Here is some text. *Here is some emphasized text.*

Here is a second-level heading

Here is some more text.

Simple HTML output

While HTML is used to define the *components* of a web page, cascading style sheets (CSS) are used to define the *styles* of the components on a page. The use of CSS allows the style of a website to be set and stay consistent throughout. For example, if the designer wanted all first-level headings (h1) to be blue and centered, he or she could set the "h1" style to match. The following example shows how this might look.

```
<style>
h1
{
color:blue;
text-align:center;
}
</style>
<h1>This is a first-level heading</h1>
Here is some text. <em>Here is some emphasized text.</em>
<h2>This is a second-level heading</h2>
Here is some more text.
```

HTML with CSS

This is a first-level heading

Here is some text. *Here is some emphasized text.*

This is a second-level heading

Here is some more text.

HTML with CSS output

The combination of HTML and CSS can be used to create a wide variety of formats and designs and has been widely adopted by the web-design community. The standards for HTML are set by a governing body called the World Wide Web Consortium. The current version of HTML is HTML 5, which includes new standards for video, audio, and drawing.

When developers create a website, they do not write it out manually in a text editor. Instead, they use web design tools that generate the HTML and CSS for them. Tools such as Adobe Dreamweaver allow the designer to create a web page that includes images and interactive elements without writing a single line of code. However, professional web designers still need to learn HTML and CSS in order to have full control over the web pages they are developing.

Build vs. Buy

When an organization decides that a new software program needs to be developed, they must determine if it makes more sense to build it themselves or to purchase it from an outside company. This is the "build vs. buy" decision.

There are many advantages to purchasing software from an outside company. First, it is generally less expensive to purchase a software package than to build it. Second, when a software package is purchased, it is available much more quickly than if the package is built in-house. Software applications can take months or years to build; a purchased package can be up and running within a month. A purchased package has already been tested and many of the bugs have already been worked out. It is the role of a systems integrator to make various purchased systems and the existing systems at the organization work together.

There are also disadvantages to purchasing software. First, the same software you are using can be used by your competitors. If a company is trying to differentiate itself based on a business process that is in that purchased software, it will have a hard time doing so if its competitors use the same software. Another disadvantage to purchasing software is the process of customization. If you purchase a software package from a vendor and then customize it, you will have to manage those customizations every time the vendor provides an upgrade. This can become an administrative headache, to say the least!

Even if an organization determines to buy software, it still makes sense to go through many of the same analyses that they would do if they were going to build it themselves. This is an important decision that could have a long-term strategic impact on the organization.

Web Services

As we saw in chapter 3, the move to cloud computing has allowed software to be looked at as a service. One option companies have these days is to license functions provided by other companies instead of writing the code themselves. These are called web services, and they can greatly simplify the addition of functionality to a website.

For example, suppose a company wishes to provide a map showing the location of someone who has called their support line. By utilizing Google Maps API web services, they can build a Google Map right into their application. Or a shoe company could make it easier for its retailers to sell shoes online by providing a shoe-size web service that the retailers could embed right into their website.

Web services can blur the lines between "build vs. buy." Companies can choose to build a software application themselves but then purchase functionality from vendors to supplement their system.

End-User Computing

In many organizations, application development is not limited to the programmers and analysts in the information-technology department. Especially in larger organizations, other departments develop their own department-specific applications. The people who build these are not necessarily trained in programming or application development, but they tend to be adept with computers. A person, for example, who is skilled in a particular software package, such as a spreadsheet or database package, may be called upon to build smaller applications for use by his or her own department. This phenomenon is referred to as end-user development, or end-user computing.

End-user computing can have many advantages for an organization. First, it brings the development of applications closer to those who will use them. Because IT departments are sometimes quite backlogged, it also provides a means to have software created more quickly. Many organizations encourage end-user computing to reduce the strain on the IT department.

End-user computing does have its disadvantages as well. If departments within an organization are developing their own applications, the organization may end up with several applications that perform similar functions, which is inefficient, since it is a duplication of effort. Sometimes, these different versions of the same application end up providing different results, bringing confusion when departments interact. These applications are often developed by someone with little or no formal training in programming. In these cases, the software developed can have problems that then have to be resolved by the IT department.

End-user computing can be beneficial to an organization, but it should be managed. The IT department should set guidelines and provide tools for the departments who want to create their own solutions. Communication between departments will go a long way towards successful use of end-user computing.

Sidebar: Building a Mobile App

In many ways, building an application for a mobile device is exactly the same as building an application for a traditional computer. Understanding the requirements for the application, designing the interface, working with users – all of these steps still need to be carried out.

So what's different about building an application for a mobile device? In some ways, mobile applications are more limited. An application running on a mobile device must be designed to be functional on a smaller screen. Mobile applications should be designed to use fingers as the primary pointing device. Mobile devices generally have less available memory, storage space, and processing power.

Mobile applications also have many advantages over applications built for traditional computers. Mobile applications have access to the functionality of the mobile device, which usually includes features such as geolocation data, messaging, the camera, and even a gyroscope.

One of the most important questions regarding development for mobile devices is this: Do we want to develop an app at all? A mobile app is an expensive proposition, and it will only run on one type of mobile device at a time. For example, if you create an iPhone app, users with Android phones are out of luck. Each app takes several thousand dollars to create, so this may not be the best use of your funds.

Many organizations are moving away from developing a specific app for a mobile device and are instead making their websites more functional on mobile devices. Using a web-design framework called responsive design, a website can be made highly functional no matter what type of device is browsing it. With a responsive website, images resize themselves based on the size of the device's screen, and text flows and sizes itself properly for optimal viewing. You can find out more about responsive design here.

Implementation Methodologies

Once a new system is developed (or purchased), the organization must determine the best method for implementing it. Convincing a group of people to learn and use a new system can be a very difficult process. Using new software, and the business processes it gives rise to, can have far-reaching effects within the organization.

There are several different methodologies an organization can adopt to implement a new system. Four of the most popular are listed below.

- Direct cutover. In the direct-cutover implementation methodology, the organization selects a particular date that the old system is not going to be used anymore. On that date, the users begin using the new system and the old system is unavailable. The advantages to using this methodology are that it is very fast and the least expensive. However, this method is the riskiest as well. If the new system has an operational problem or if the users are not properly prepared, it could prove disastrous for the organization.

- Pilot implementation. In this methodology, a subset of the organization (called a pilot group) starts using the new system before the rest of the organization. This has a smaller impact on the company and allows the support team to focus on a smaller group of individuals.

- Parallel operation. With parallel operation, the old and new systems are used simultaneously for a limited period of time. This method is the least risky because the old system is still being used while the new system is essentially being tested. However, this is by far the most expensive methodology since work is duplicated and support is needed for both systems in full.

- Phased implementation. In phased implementation, different functions of the new application are used as functions from the old system are turned off. This approach allows an organization to slowly move from one system to another.

Which of these implementation methodologies to use depends on the complexity and importance of the old and new systems.

Change Management

As new systems are brought online and old systems are phased out, it becomes important to manage the way change is implemented in the organization. Change should never be introduced in a vacuum. The organization should be sure to communicate proposed changes before they happen and plan to minimize the impact of the change that will occur after implementation. Change management is a critical component of IT oversight.

Maintenance

Once a new system has been introduced, it enters the maintenance phase. In this phase, the system is in production and is being used by the organization. While the system is no longer actively being developed, changes need to be made when bugs are found or new features are requested. During the maintenance phase, IT management must ensure that the system continues to stay aligned with business priorities and continues to run well.

Summary

Software development is about so much more than programming. Developing new software applications requires several steps, from the formal SDLC process to more informal processes such as agile programming or lean methodologies. Programming languages have evolved from very low-level machine-specific languages to higher-level languages that allow a programmer to write software for a wide variety of machines. Most programmers work with software development tools that provide them with integrated components to make the software development process more efficient. For some organizations, building their own software applications does not make the most sense; instead, they choose to purchase software built by a third party to save development costs and speed implementation. In end-user computing, software development happens outside the information technology department. When implementing new software applications, there are several different types of implementation methodologies that must be considered.

Study Questions

1. What are the steps in the SDLC methodology?
2. What is RAD software development?

3. What makes the lean methodology unique?

4. What are three differences between second-generation and third-generation languages?

5. Why would an organization consider building its own software application if it is cheaper to buy one?

6. What is responsive design?

7. What is the relationship between HTML and CSS in website design?

8. What is the difference between the pilot implementation methodology and the parallel implementation methodology?

9. What is change management?

10. What are the four different implementation methodologies?

Exercises

1. Which software-development methodology would be best if an organization needed to develop a software tool for a small group of users in the marketing department? Why? Which implementation methodology should they use? Why?

2. Doing your own research, find three programming languages and categorize them in these areas: generation, compiled vs. interpreted, procedural vs. object-oriented.

3. Some argue that HTML is not a programming language. Doing your own research, find three arguments for why it is not a programming language and three arguments for why it is.

4. Read more about responsive design using the link given in the text. Provide the links to three websites that use responsive design and explain how they demonstrate responsive-design behavior.

Part 3: Information Systems Beyond the Organization

Chapter 11: Globalization and the Digital Divide

Learning Objectives

Upon successful completion of this chapter, you will be able to:

- explain the concept of globalization;
- describe the role of information technology in globalization;
- identify the issues experienced by firms as they face a global economy; and
- define the digital divide and explain Nielsen's three stages of the digital divide.

Introduction

The Internet has wired the world. Today it is just as simple to communicate with someone on the other side of the world as it is to talk to someone next door. In this chapter, we will look at the implications of globalization and the impact it is having on the world.

What Is Globalization?

Globalization is the term used to refer to the integration of goods, services, and culture among the nations of the world. Globalization is not necessarily a new phenomenon; in many ways, we have been experiencing globalization since the days of European colonization. Further advances in telecommunication and transportation technologies accelerated globalization. The advent of the the worldwide Internet has made all nations next-door neighbors.

The Internet is truly a worldwide phenomenon. As of 2012, the Internet was being used in over 150 countries by a staggering 2.4 billion people worldwide, and growing.[1] From its initial beginnings in the United States in the 1970s to the development of the World Wide Web in the 1990s to the social networks and e-commerce of today, the Internet has continued to increase the integration between countries, making globalization a fact of life for citizens all over the world.

1. http://internetworldstats.com/

WORLD INTERNET USAGE AND POPULATION STATISTICS
As of June 30, 2012

World Regions	Population (2012 Est.)	Internet Users Dec. 31, 2000	Internet Users Latest Data	Penetration (% Population)	Growth 2000-2012	Users % of Table
Africa	1,073,380,925	4,514,400	167,335,676	15.6%	3,606.7%	7.0%
Asia	3,922,066,987	114,304,000	1,076,681,059	27.5%	841.9%	44.8%
Europe	820,918,446	105,096,093	518,512,109	63.2%	393.4%	21.5%
Middle East	223,608,203	3,284,800	90,000,455	40.2%	2,639.9%	3.7%
North America	348,280,154	108,096,800	273,785,413	78.6%	153.3%	11.4%
Latin America / Caribbean	593,688,638	18,068,919	254,915,745	42.9%	1,310.8%	10.6%
Oceania / Australia	35,903,569	7,620,480	24,287,919	67.6%	218.7%	1.0%
WORLD TOTAL	7,017,846,922	360,985,492	2,405,518,376	34.3%	566.4%	100.0%

Source: Internet World Stats

The Network Society

In 1996, social-sciences researcher Manuel Castells published *The Rise of the Network Society,* in which he identified new ways in which economic activity was being organized around the networks that the new telecommunication technologies have provided. This new, global economic activity was different from the past, because "it is an economy with the capacity to work as a unit in real time on a planetary scale."[2] We are now into this network society, where we are all connected on a global scale.

The World Is Flat

In 2005, Thomas Friedman's seminal book, *The World Is Flat,* was published. In this book, Friedman unpacks the impacts that the personal computer, the Internet, and communication software have had on business, specifically the impact they have had on globalization. He begins the book by defining the three eras of globalization[3]:

- "Globalization 1.0″ occurred from 1492 until about 1800. In this era, globalization was centered around countries. It was about how much horsepower, wind power, and steam power a country had and how creatively it was deployed. The world shrank from size "large" to size "medium."

- "Globalization 2.0″ occurred from about 1800 until 2000, interrupted only by the two World Wars. In this era, the dynamic force driving change was multinational companies. The world shrank from size "medium" to size "small."

- "Globalization 3.0″ is our current era, beginning in the year 2000. The convergence of the personal computer, fiber-optic Internet connections, and software has created a "flat-world platform" that allows small groups and even individuals to go global. The world has shrunk from size "small" to size "tiny."

---

2. Manuel Castells. 2000. The Rise of the Network Society (2nd ed.). Blackwell Publishers, Inc., Cambridge, MA, USA.

3. Friedman, T. L. (2005). The world is flat: A brief history of the twenty-first century. New York: Farrar, Straus and Giroux.

According to Friedman, this third era of globalization was brought about, in many respects, by information technology. Some of the specific technologies he lists include:

- *The graphical user interface for the personal computer popularized in the late 1980s.* Before the graphical user interface, using a computer was relatively difficult. By making the personal computer something that anyone could use, it became commonplace very quickly. Friedman points out that this digital storage of content made people much more productive and, as the Internet evolved, made it simpler to communicate content worldwide.

- *The build-out of the Internet infrastructure during the dot-com boom during the late-1990s.* During the late 1990s, telecommunications companies laid thousands of miles of fiber-optic cable all over the world, turning network communications into a commodity. At the same time, the Internet protocols, such as SMTP (e-mail), HTML (web pages), and TCP/IP (network communications) became standards that were available for free and used by everyone.

- *The introduction of software to automate and integrate business processes.* As the Internet continued to grow and become the dominant form of communication, it became essential to build on the standards developed earlier so that the websites and applications running on the Internet would work well together. Friedman calls this "workflow software," by which he means software that allows people to work together more easily, and allows different software packages and databases to integrate with each other more easily. Examples include payment-processing systems and shipping calculators.

These three technologies came together in the late 1990s to create a "platform for global collaboration." Once these technologies were in place, they continued to evolve. Friedman also points out a couple more technologies that have contributed to the flat-world platform – the open-source movement (see chapter 10) and the advent of mobile technologies.

The World Is Flat was published in 2005. Since then, we have seen even more growth in information technologies that have contributed to global collaborations. We will discuss current and future trends in chapter 13.

The Global Firm

The new era of globalization allows any business to become international. By accessing this new platform of technologies, Castells's vision of working as a unit in real time on a planetary scale can be a reality. Some of the advantages of this include the following:

- The ability to locate expertise and labor around the world. Instead of drawing employees from their local area, organizations can now hire people from the global labor pool. This also allows organizations to pay a lower labor cost for the same work based on the prevailing wage in different countries.

- The ability to operate 24 hours a day. With employees in different time zones all around the world, an organization can literally operate around the clock, handing off work on projects from one part of the world to another. Businesses can also keep their digital storefront (their website) open all the time.

- A larger market for their products. Once a product is being sold online, it is available for purchase from a worldwide consumer base. Even if a company's products do not appeal beyond its own country's borders, being online has also made the product more visible to consumers within that country.

In order to fully take advantage of these new capabilities, companies need to understand that there are also challenges in dealing with employees and customers from different cultures. Some of these challenges include:

- Infrastructure differences. Each country has its own infrastructure, many of which are not of the same quality as the US infrastructure (average 4.60 MBps). For every South Korea (16 MBps average speed) there is an Egypt (0.83 MBps) or an India (0.82 MBps). A business cannot depend on every country it deals with having the same Internet speeds. See the sidebar called "How Does My Internet Speed Compare?"

- Labor laws and regulations. Different countries (even different states in the United States) have different laws and regulations. A company that wants to hire employees from other countries must understand the different regulations and concerns.

- Legal restrictions. Many countries have restrictions on what can be sold or how a product can be advertised. It is important for a business to understand what is allowed. For example, in Germany, it is illegal to sell anything Nazi related; in China, it is illegal to put anything sexually suggestive online.

- Language, customs, and preferences. Every country has its own (or several) unique culture(s), which a business must consider when trying to market a product there. Additionally, different countries have different preferences. For example, in some parts of the world, people prefer to eat their french fries with mayonnaise instead of ketchup; in other parts of the world, specific hand gestures (such as the thumbs-up) are offensive.

- International shipping. Shipping products between countries in a timely manner can be challenging. Inconsistent address formats, dishonest customs agents, and prohibitive shipping costs are all factors that must be considered when trying to deliver products internationally.

Because of these challenges, many businesses choose not to expand globally, either for labor or for customers. Whether a business has its own website or relies on a third-party, such as Amazon or eBay, the question of whether or not to globalize must be carefully considered.

Sidebar: How Does My Internet Speed Compare?

How does your Internet speed compare with others in your state, country, or around the world? The chart below shows how Internet speeds compare in different countries. You can find the full list of countries by going to this article (http://royal.pingdom.com/2010/11/12/real-connection-speeds-for-internet-users-across-the-world/). You can also compare the evolution of Internet speeds among countries by using this tool (http://www.akamai.com/stateoftheinternet/).

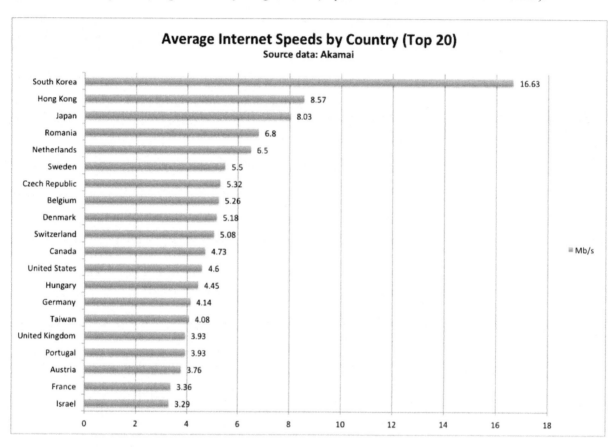

Internet speeds by country. Click to enlarge.

So how does your own Internet speed compare? There are many online tools you can use to determine the speed at which you are connected. One of the most trusted sites is speedtest.net, where you can test both your download speeds and upload speeds.

The Digital Divide

As the Internet continues to make inroads across the world, it is also creating a separation between those who have access to this global network and those who do not. This separation is called the "digital divide" and is of great concern. An article in *Crossroads* puts it this way[4]:

> Adopted by the ACM Council in 1992, the ACM Code of Ethics and Professional Conduct focuses on issues involving the Digital Divide that could prevent certain categories of people — those from low-income households, senior citizens, single-parent children, the undereducated,

---

4. Kibum Kim. 2005. Challenges in HCI: digital divide. *Crossroads* 12, 2 (December 2005), 2-2. DOI=10.1145/1144375.1144377
  http://doi.acm.org/10.1145/1144375.1144377

minorities, and residents of rural areas — from receiving adequate access to the wide variety of resources offered by computer technology. This Code of Ethics positions the use of computers as a fundamental ethical consideration: "In a fair society, all individuals would have equal opportunity to participate in, or benefit from, the use of computer resources regardless of race, sex, religion, age, disability, national origin, or other similar factors." This article summarizes the digital divide in its various forms, and analyzes reasons for the growing inequality in people's access to Internet services. It also describes how society can bridge the digital divide: the serious social gap between information "haves" and "have-nots."

The digital divide can occur between countries, regions, or even neighborhoods. In many US cities, there are pockets with little or no Internet access, while just a few miles away high-speed broadband is common.

Solutions to the digital divide have had mixed success over the years. Many times, just providing Internet access and/or computing devices is not enough to bring true Internet access to a country, region, or neighborhood.

One Laptop per Child

One attempt to repair the digital divide was the One Laptop per Child effort. As stated on the organization's website, "The mission of One Laptop per Child (OLPC) is to empower the children of developing countries to learn by providing one connected laptop to every school-age child. In order to accomplish our goal, we need people who believe in what we're doing and want to help make education for the world's children a priority, not a privilege."[5] Announced to great fanfare in 2005 by Nicholas Negroponte, the OLPC project seemed destined for success.

The XO laptop. Click to enlarge. (CC-BY: Mike McGregor)

The centerpiece of the project was the laptop itself: an inexpensive computer designed to withstand a lot of punishment. It utilized a revolutionary "mesh" network, allowing the laptops to act as repeaters, extending a Wi-Fi network far beyond their normal range. They also used minimal power, making them practical for remote areas with limited access to the electrical grid.

Unfortunately, the OLPC project failed to live up to expectations, running into many of the problems related to globalization discussed above: different cultures, corruption, and competition. In an article that examined the success and failures of OLPC, the authors state, "Expecting a laptop to cause such a revolutionary change showed a degree of naivete, even for an organization with the best of intentions and the smartest of people."[6] Today, OLPC is evolving their methods and their technology, trying to deliver an OLPC tablet computer.

5. http://laptop.org/en/vision/mission/
6. One Laptop Per Child: Vision vs. Reality By Kenneth L. Kraemer, Jason Dedrick, Prakul Sharma Communications of the ACM, Vol. 52 No. 6, Pages 66-73

A New Understanding of the Digital Divide

In 2006, web-usability consultant Jakob Nielsen wrote an article that got to the heart of our understanding of this problem. In his article, he breaks the digital divide up into three stages: the economic divide, the usability divide, and the empowerment divide[7].

What is usually called the digital divide is, in Nielsen's terms, the *economic divide*: the idea that some people can afford to have a computer and Internet access while others cannot. Because of Moore's Law (see chapter 2), the price of hardware has continued to drop and, at this point, we can now access digital technologies, such as smartphones, for very little. This fact, Nielsen asserts, means that for all intents and purposes, the economic divide is a moot point and we should not focus our resources on solving it.

The *usability divide* is concerned with the fact that "technology remains so complicated that many people couldn't use a computer even if they got one for free." And even for those who can use a computer, accessing all the benefits of having one is beyond their understanding. Included in this group are those with low literacy and seniors. According to Nielsen, we know how to help these users, but we are not doing it because there is little profit in doing so.

The *empowerment divide* is the most difficult to solve. It is concerned with how we use technology to empower ourselves. Very few users truly understand the power that digital technologies can give them. In his article, Nielsen explains that his (and others') research has shown that very few users contribute content to the Internet, use advanced search, or can even distinguish paid search ads from organic search results. Many people will limit what they can do online by accepting the basic, default settings of their computer and not work to understand how they can truly be empowered.

Understanding the digital divide using these three stages provides a more nuanced view of how we can work to alleviate it. While efforts such as One Laptop per Child are an excellent start, more work needs to be done to address the second and third stages of the digital divide for a more holistic solution.

Sidebar: Using Gaming to Bridge the Digital Divide

Paul Kim, the Assistant Dean and Chief Technology Officer of the Stanford Graduate School of Education, designed a project to address the digital divide for children in developing countries. [8] In their project, the researchers wanted to understand if children can adopt and teach themselves mobile learning technology, without help from teachers or other adults, and the processes and factors involved in this phenomenon. The researchers developed a mobile device called TeacherMate, which contained a game designed to help children learn math. The unique part of this research was that the researchers interacted directly with the children; they did not channel the mobile devices through the teachers or the schools. Another important factor to consider: in order to understand the context of the children's educational environment, the researchers began the project by working with parents and local nonprofits six months before their visit. While the results of this research are too detailed to go into here, it can be said that the researchers found that children can, indeed, adopt and teach themselves mobile learning technologies.

What makes this research so interesting when thinking about the digital divide is that the researchers found that, in order to be effective, they had to customize their technology and tailor their implementation to the specific group they were trying to reach. One of their conclusions stated the following:

7. http://www.nngroup.com/articles/digital-divide-the-three-stages/

8. Kim, P., Buckner, E., Makany, T., & Kim, H. (2011). A comparative analysis of a game-based mobile learning model in low-socioeconomic communities of India. International Journal of Educational Development. doi:10.1016/j.ijedudev.2011.05.008.

Considering the rapid advancement of technology today, mobile learning options for future projects will only increase. Consequently, researchers must continue to investigate their impact; we believe there is a specific need for more in-depth studies on ICT [information and communication technology] design variations to meet different challenges of different localities.

To read more about Dr. Kim's project, locate the paper referenced in this sidebar.

Summary

Information technology has driven change on a global scale. As documented by Castells and Friedman, technology has given us the ability to integrate with people all over the world using digital tools. These tools have allowed businesses to broaden their labor pools, their markets, and even their operating hours. But they have also brought many new complications for businesses, which now must understand regulations, preferences, and cultures from many different nations. This new globalization has also exacerbated the digital divide. Nielsen has suggested that the digital divide consists of three stages (economic, usability, and empowerment), of which the economic stage is virtually solved.

Study Questions

1. What does the term *globalization* mean?

2. How does Friedman define the three eras of globalization?

3. Which technologies have had the biggest effect on globalization?

4. What are some of the advantages brought about by globalization?

5. What are the challenges of globalization?

6. What does the term *digital divide* mean?

7. What are Jakob Nielsen's three stages of the digital divide?

8. What was one of the key points of *The Rise of the Network Society*?

9. Which country has the highest average Internet speed? How does your country compare?

10. What is the OLPC project? Has it been successful?

Exercises

1. Compare the concept of Friedman's "Globalization 3.0" with Nielsen empowerment stage of the digital divide.

2. Do some original research to determine some of the regulations that a US company may have to consider before doing business in one of the following countries: China, Germany, Saudi Arabia, Turkey.

3. Go to speedtest.net to determine your Internet speed. Compare your speed at home to the Internet speed at two other locations, such as your school, place of employment, or local coffee shop. Write up a one-page summary that compares these locations.

4. Give one example of the digital divide and describe what you would do to address it.

5. How did the research conducted by Paul Kim address the three levels of the digital divide?

Chapter 12: The Ethical and Legal Implications of Information Systems

Learning Objectives

Upon successful completion of this chapter, you will be able to:

- describe what the term *information systems ethics* means;
- explain what a code of ethics is and describe the advantages and disadvantages;
- define the term *intellectual property* and explain the protections provided by copyright, patent, and trademark; and
- describe the challenges that information technology brings to individual privacy.

Introduction

Information systems have had an impact far beyond the world of business. New technologies create new situations that we have never dealt with before. How do we handle the new capabilities that these devices empower us with? What new laws are going to be needed to protect us from ourselves? This chapter will kick off with a discussion of the impact of information systems on how we behave (ethics). This will be followed with the new legal structures being put in place, with a focus on intellectual property and privacy.

Information Systems Ethics

The term *ethics* is defined as "a set of moral principles" or "the principles of conduct governing an individual or a group."[1] Since the dawn of civilization, the study of ethics and their impact has fascinated mankind. But what do ethics have to do with information systems?

The introduction of new technology can have a profound effect on human behavior. New technologies give us capabilities that we did not have before, which in turn create environments and situations that have not been specifically addressed in ethical terms. Those who master new technologies gain new power; those who cannot or do not master them may lose power. In 1913, Henry Ford implemented the first moving assembly line to create his Model T cars. While this was a great step forward technologically (and economically), the assembly line reduced the value of human beings in the production process. The development of the atomic bomb concentrated unimaginable power in the hands of one government, who then had to wrestle with the decision to use it. Today's digital technologies have created new categories of ethical dilemmas.

For example, the ability to anonymously make perfect copies of digital music has tempted many music fans to download copyrighted music for their own use without making payment to the music's owner. Many of those who would never have walked into a music store and stolen a CD find themselves with dozens of illegally downloaded albums.

---

1. http://www.merriam-webster.com/dictionary/ethics

Digital technologies have given us the ability to aggregate information from multiple sources to create profiles of people. What would have taken weeks of work in the past can now be done in seconds, allowing private organizations and governments to know more about individuals than at any time in history. This information has value, but also chips away at the privacy of consumers and citizens.

Code of Ethics

One method for navigating new ethical waters is a code of ethics. A code of ethics is a document that outlines a set of acceptable behaviors for a professional or social group; generally, it is agreed to by all members of the group. The document details different actions that are considered appropriate and inappropriate.

A good example of a code of ethics is the *Code of Ethics and Professional Conduct* of the Association for Computing Machinery,[2] an organization of computing professionals that includes academics, researchers, and practitioners. Here is a quote from the preamble:

> Commitment to ethical professional conduct is expected of every member (voting members, associate members, and student members) of the Association for Computing Machinery (ACM).
>
> This Code, consisting of 24 imperatives formulated as statements of personal responsibility, identifies the elements of such a commitment. It contains many, but not all, issues professionals are likely to face. Section 1 outlines fundamental ethical considerations, while Section 2 addresses additional, more specific considerations of professional conduct. Statements in Section 3 pertain more specifically to individuals who have a leadership role, whether in the workplace or in a volunteer capacity such as with organizations like ACM. Principles involving compliance with this Code are given in Section 4.

In the ACM's code, you will find many straightforward ethical instructions, such as the admonition to be honest and trustworthy. But because this is also an organization of professionals that focuses on computing, there are more specific admonitions that relate directly to information technology:

- No one should enter or use another's computer system, software, or data files without permission. One must always have appropriate approval before using system resources, including communication ports, file space, other system peripherals, and computer time.

- Designing or implementing systems that deliberately or inadvertently demean individuals or groups is ethically unacceptable.

- Organizational leaders are responsible for ensuring that computer systems enhance, not degrade, the quality of working life. When implementing a computer system, organizations must consider the personal and professional development, physical safety, and human dignity of all workers. Appropriate human-computer ergonomic standards should be considered in system design and in the workplace.

One of the major advantages of creating a code of ethics is that it clarifies the acceptable standards of behavior for a professional group. The varied backgrounds and experiences of the members of a group

2. ACM Code of Ethics and Professional Conduct Adopted by ACM Council 10/16/92.

lead to a variety of ideas regarding what is acceptable behavior. While to many the guidelines may seem obvious, having these items detailed provides clarity and consistency. Explicitly stating standards communicates the common guidelines to everyone in a clear manner.

Having a code of ethics can also have some drawbacks. First of all, a code of ethics does not have legal authority; in other words, breaking a code of ethics is not a crime in itself. So what happens if someone violates one of the guidelines? Many codes of ethics include a section that describes how such situations will be handled. In many cases, repeated violations of the code result in expulsion from the group.

In the case of ACM: "Adherence of professionals to a code of ethics is largely a voluntary matter. However, if a member does not follow this code by engaging in gross misconduct, membership in ACM may be terminated." Expulsion from ACM may not have much of an impact on many individuals, since membership in ACM is usually not a requirement for employment. However, expulsion from other organizations, such as a state bar organization or medical board, could carry a huge impact.

Another possible disadvantage of a code of ethics is that there is always a chance that important issues will arise that are not specifically addressed in the code. Technology is quickly changing, and a code of ethics might not be updated often enough to keep up with all of the changes. A good code of ethics, however, is written in a broad enough fashion that it can address the ethical issues of potential changes to technology while the organization behind the code makes revisions.

Finally, a code of ethics could have also be a disadvantage in that it may not entirely reflect the ethics or morals of every member of the group. Organizations with a diverse membership may have internal conflicts as to what is acceptable behavior. For example, there may be a difference of opinion on the consumption of alcoholic beverages at company events. In such cases, the organization must make a choice about the importance of addressing a specific behavior in the code.

Sidebar: Acceptable Use Policies

Many organizations that provide technology services to a group of constituents or the public require agreement to an acceptable use policy (AUP) before those services can be accessed. Similar to a code of ethics, this policy outlines what is allowed and what is not allowed while someone is using the organization's services. An everyday example of this is the terms of service that must be agreed to before using the public Wi-Fi at Starbucks, McDonald's, or even a university. Here is an example of an acceptable use policy from Virginia Tech.

Just as with a code of ethics, these acceptable use policies specify what is allowed and what is not allowed. Again, while some of the items listed are obvious to most, others are not so obvious:

- "Borrowing" someone else's login ID and password is prohibited.
- Using the provided access for commercial purposes, such as hosting your own business website, is not allowed.
- Sending out unsolicited email to a large group of people is prohibited.

Also as with codes of ethics, violations of these policies have various consequences. In most cases, such as with Wi-Fi, violating the acceptable use policy will mean that you will lose your access to the resource. While losing access to Wi-Fi at Starbucks may not have a lasting impact, a university student getting banned from the university's Wi-Fi (or possibly all network resources) could have a large impact.

Intellectual Property

One of the domains that have been deeply impacted by digital technologies is the domain of intellectual property. Digital technologies have driven a rise in new intellectual property claims and made it much more difficult to defend intellectual property.

Intellectual property is defined as "property (as an idea, invention, or process) that derives from the work of the mind or intellect."[3] This could include creations such as song lyrics, a computer program, a new type of toaster, or even a sculpture.

Practically speaking, it is very difficult to protect an idea. Instead, intellectual property laws are written to protect the tangible results of an idea. In other words, just coming up with a song in your head is not protected, but if you write it down it can be protected.

Protection of intellectual property is important because it gives people an incentive to be creative. Innovators with great ideas will be more likely to pursue those ideas if they have a clear understanding of how they will benefit. In the US Constitution, Article 8, Section 8, the authors saw fit to recognize the importance of protecting creative works:

> Congress shall have the power . . . To promote the Progress of Science and useful Arts, by securing for limited Times to Authors and Inventors the exclusive Right to their respective Writings and Discoveries.

An important point to note here is the "limited time" qualification. While protecting intellectual property is important because of the incentives it provides, it is also necessary to limit the amount of benefit that can be received and allow the results of ideas to become part of the public domain.

Outside of the US, intellectual property protections vary. You can find out more about a specific country's intellectual property laws by visiting the World Intellectual Property Organization.

In the following sections we will review three of the best-known intellectual property protections: copyright, patent, and trademark.

Copyright

Copyright is the protection given to songs, computer programs, books, and other creative works; any work that has an "author" can be copyrighted. Under the terms of copyright, the author of a work controls what can be done with the work, including:

- Who can make copies of the work.
- Who can make derivative works from the original work.
- Who can perform the work publicly.
- Who can display the work publicly.
- Who can distribute the work.

---

3. http://www.merriam-webster.com/dictionary/intellectual%20property

Many times, a work is not owned by an individual but is instead owned by a publisher with whom the original author has an agreement. In return for the rights to the work, the publisher will market and distribute the work and then pay the original author a portion of the proceeds.

Copyright protection lasts for the life of the original author plus seventy years. In the case of a copyrighted work owned by a publisher or another third party, the protection lasts for ninety-five years from the original creation date. For works created before 1978, the protections vary slightly. You can see the full details on copyright protections by reviewing the Copyright Basics document available at the US Copyright Office's website.

Obtaining Copyright Protection

In the United States, a copyright is obtained by the simple act of creating the original work. In other words, when an author writes down that song, makes that film, or designs that program, he or she automatically has the copyright. However, for a work that will be used commercially, it is advisable to register for a copyright with the US Copyright Office. A registered copyright is needed in order to bring legal action against someone who has used a work without permission.

First Sale Doctrine

If an artist creates a painting and sells it to a collector who then, for whatever reason, proceeds to destroy it, does the original artist have any recourse? What if the collector, instead of destroying it, begins making copies of it and sells them? Is this allowed? The first sale doctrine is a part of copyright law that addresses this, as shown below[4]:

> The first sale doctrine, codified at 17 U.S.C. § 109, provides that an individual who knowingly purchases a copy of a copyrighted work from the copyright holder receives the right to sell, display or otherwise dispose of *that particular copy*, notwithstanding the interests of the copyright owner.

So, in our examples, the copyright owner has no recourse if the collector destroys her artwork. But the collector does not have the right to make copies of the artwork.

Fair Use

Another important provision within copyright law is that of fair use. Fair use is a limitation on copyright law that allows for the use of protected works without prior authorization in specific cases. For example, if a teacher wanted to discuss a current event in her class, she could pass out copies of a copyrighted news story to her students without first getting permission. Fair use is also what allows a student to quote a small portion of a copyrighted work in a research paper.

Unfortunately, the specific guidelines for what is considered fair use and what constitutes copyright violation are not well defined. Fair use is a well-known and respected concept and will only be challenged when copyright holders feel that the integrity or market value of their work is being threatened. The following four factors are considered when determining if something constitutes fair use: [5]

1. The purpose and character of the use, including whether such use is of commercial nature or is for nonprofit educational purposes;

4. http://www.justice.gov/usao/eousa/foia_reading_room/usam/title9/crm01854.htm

5. http://www.copyright.gov/fls/fl102.html

2. The nature of the copyrighted work;

3. The amount and substantiality of the portion used in relation to the copyrighted work as a whole;

4. The effect of the use upon the potential market for, or value of, the copyrighted work.

If you are ever considering using a copyrighted work as part of something you are creating, you may be able to do so under fair use. However, it is always best to check with the copyright owner to be sure you are staying within your rights and not infringing upon theirs.

Sidebar: The History of Copyright Law

As noted above, current copyright law grants copyright protection for seventy years after the author's death, or ninety-five years from the date of creation for a work created for hire. But it was not always this way.

The first US copyright law, which only protected books, maps, and charts, provided protection for only 14 years with a renewable term of 14 years. Over time, copyright law was revised to grant protections to other forms of creative expression, such as photography and motion pictures. Congress also saw fit to extend the length of the protections, as shown in the chart below. Today, copyright has become big business, with many businesses relying on the income from copyright-protected works for their income.

Many now think that the protections last too long. The Sonny Bono Copyright Term Extension Act has been nicknamed the "Mickey Mouse Protection Act," as it was enacted just in time to protect the copyright on the Walt Disney Company's Mickey Mouse character. Because of this term extension, many works from the 1920s and 1930s that would have been available now in the public domain are not available.

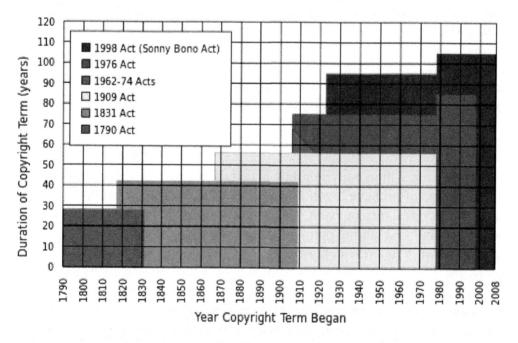

Evolution of copyright term length. (CC-BY-SA: Tom Bell)

The Digital Millennium Copyright Act

As digital technologies have changed what it means to create, copy, and distribute media, a policy vacuum has been created. In 1998, the US Congress passed the Digital Millennium Copyright Act (DMCA), which extended copyright law to take into consideration digital technologies. Two of the best-known provisions from the DMCA are the anti-circumvention provision and the "safe harbor" provision.

- The anti-circumvention provision makes it illegal to create technology to circumvent technology that has been put in place to protect a copyrighted work. This provision includes not just the creation of the technology but also the publishing of information that describes how to do it. While this provision does allow for some exceptions, it has become quite controversial and has led to a movement to have it modified.

- The "safe harbor" provision limits the liability of online service providers when someone using their services commits copyright infringement. This is the provision that allows YouTube, for example, not to be held liable when someone posts a clip from a copyrighted movie. The provision does require the online service provider to take action when they are notified of the violation (a "takedown" notice). For an example of how takedown works, here's how YouTube handles these requests: YouTube Copyright Infringement Notification.

Many think that the DMCA goes too far and ends up limiting our freedom of speech. The Electronic Frontier Foundation (EFF) is at the forefront of this battle. For example, in discussing the anti-circumvention provision, the EFF states:

> Yet the DMCA has become a serious threat that jeopardizes fair use, impedes competition and innovation, chills free expression and scientific research, and interferes with computer intrusion laws. If you circumvent DRM [digital rights management] locks for non-infringing fair uses or create the tools to do so you might be on the receiving end of a lawsuit.

Sidebar: Creative Commons

In chapter 2, we learned about open-source software. Open-source software has few or no copyright restrictions; the creators of the software publish their code and make their software available for others to use and distribute for free. This is great for software, but what about other forms of copyrighted works? If an artist or writer wants to make their works available, how can they go about doing so while still protecting the integrity of their work? Creative Commons is the solution to this problem.

Creative Commons is a nonprofit organization that provides legal tools for artists and authors. The tools offered make it simple to license artistic or literary work for others to use or distribute in a manner consistent with the author's intentions. Creative Commons licenses are indicated with the symbol ⓒ. It is important to note that Creative Commons and public domain are not the same. When something is in the public domain, it has absolutely no restrictions on its use or distribution. Works whose copyrights have expired, for example, are in the public domain.

By using a Creative Commons license, authors can control the use of their work while still making it widely accessible. By attaching a Creative Commons license to their work, a legally binding license is created. Here are some examples of these licenses:

- CC-BY: This is the least restrictive license. It lets others distribute and build upon the work, even commercially, as long as they give the author credit for the original work.
- CC-BY-SA: This license restricts the distribution of the work via the "share-alike" clause. This means that others can freely distribute and build upon the work, but they must give credit to the original author *and* they must share using the same Creative Commons license.
- CC-BY-NC: This license is the same as CC-BY but adds the restriction that no one can make money with this work. NC stands for "non-commercial."
- CC-BY-NC-ND: This license is the same as CC-BY-NC but also adds the ND restriction, which means that no derivative works may be made from the original.

These are a few of the more common licenses that can be created using the tools that Creative Commons makes available. For a full listing of the licenses and to learn much more about Creative Commons, visit their web site.

Patent

Another important form of intellectual property protection is the patent. A patent creates protection for someone who invents a new product or process. The definition of invention is quite broad and covers many different fields. Here are some examples of items receiving patents:

- circuit designs in semiconductors;
- prescription drug formulas;
- firearms;
- locks;
- plumbing;
- engines;
- coating processes; and
- business processes.

Once a patent is granted, it provides the inventor with protection from others infringing on his or her patent. A patent holder has the right to "exclude others from making, using, offering for sale, or selling the invention throughout the United States or importing the invention into the United States for a limited time in exchange for public disclosure of the invention when the patent is granted."[6]

As with copyright, patent protection lasts for a limited period of time before the invention or process enters the public domain. In the US, a patent lasts twenty years. This is why generic drugs are available to replace brand-name drugs after twenty years.

6. From the US Patent and Trademark Office, "What Is A Patent?" http://www.uspto.gov/patents/

Obtaining Patent Protection

Unlike copyright, a patent is not automatically granted when someone has an interesting idea and writes it down. In most countries, a patent application must be submitted to a government patent office. A patent will only be granted if the invention or process being submitted meets certain conditions:

- It must be original. The invention being submitted must not have been submitted before.
- It must be non-obvious. You cannot patent something that anyone could think of. For example, you could not put a pencil on a chair and try to get a patent for a pencil-holding chair.
- It must be useful. The invention being submitted must serve some purpose or have some use that would be desired.

The job of the patent office is to review patent applications to ensure that the item being submitted meets these requirements. This is not an easy job: in 2012, the US Patent Office received 576,763 patent applications and granted 276,788 patents. The current backlog for a patent approval is 18.1 months. Over the past fifty years, the number of patent applications has risen from just 100,000 a year to almost 600,000; digital technologies are driving much of this innovation.

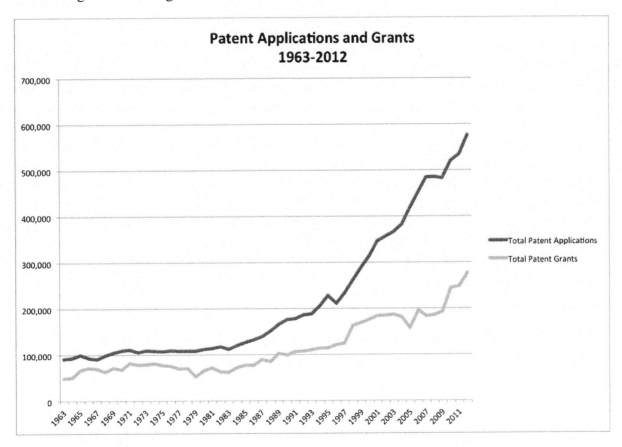

Increase in patent applications, 1963–2012 (Source: US Patent and Trademark Office)

Sidebar: What Is a Patent Troll?

The advent of digital technologies has led to a large increase in patent filings and therefore a large number of patents being granted. Once a patent is granted, it is up to the owner of the patent to enforce it; if someone is found to be using the invention without permission, the patent holder has the right to sue to force that person to stop and to collect damages.

The rise in patents has led to a new form of profiteering called patent trolling. A patent troll is a person or organization who gains the rights to a patent but does not actually make the invention that the patent protects. Instead, the patent troll searches for those who are illegally using the invention in some way and sues them. In many cases, the infringement being alleged is questionable at best. For example, companies have been sued for using Wi-Fi or for scanning documents, technologies that have been on the market for many years.

Recently, the US government has begun taking action against patent trolls. Several pieces of legislation are working their way through Congress that will, if enacted, limit the ability of patent trolls to threaten innovation. You can learn a lot more about patent trolls by listening to a detailed investigation conducted by the radio program *This American Life,* by clicking this link.

Trademark

A trademark is a word, phrase, logo, shape or sound that identifies a source of goods or services. For example, the Nike "Swoosh," the Facebook "f", and Apple's apple (with a bite taken out of it) are all trademarked. The concept behind trademarks is to protect the consumer. Imagine going to the local shopping center to purchase a specific item from a specific store and finding that there are several stores all with the same name!

Two types of trademarks exist – a common-law trademark and a registered trademark. As with copyright, an organization will automatically receive a trademark if a word, phrase, or logo is being used in the normal course of business (subject to some restrictions, discussed below). A common-law trademark is designated by placing "TM" next to the trademark. A registered trademark is one that has been examined, approved, and registered with the trademark office, such as the Patent and Trademark Office in the US. A registered trademark has the circle-R (®) placed next to the trademark.

While most any word, phrase, logo, shape, or sound can be trademarked, there are a few limitations. A trademark will not hold up legally if it meets one or more of the following conditions:

1. The trademark is likely to cause confusion with a mark in a registration or prior application.
2. The trademark is merely descriptive for the goods/services. For example, trying to register the trademark "blue" for a blue product you are selling will not pass muster.
3. The trademark is a geographic term.
4. The trademark is a surname. You will not be allowed to trademark "Smith's Bookstore."
5. The trademark is ornamental as applied to the goods. For example, a repeating flower pattern that is a design on a plate cannot be trademarked.

As long as an organization uses its trademark and defends it against infringement, the protection afforded by it does not expire. Because of this, many organizations defend their trademark against other companies whose branding even only slightly copies their trademark. For example, Chick-fil-A has trademarked the phrase "Eat Mor Chikin" and has vigorously defended it against a small business using the slogan "Eat More Kale." Coca-Cola has trademarked the contour shape of its bottle and will bring legal action against any company using a bottle design similar to theirs. As an example of trademarks that have been diluted and have now lost their protection in the US are "aspirin" (originally trademarked by Bayer), "escalator" (originally trademarked by Otis), and "yo-yo" (originally trademarked by Duncan).

Information Systems and Intellectual Property

The rise of information systems has forced us to rethink how we deal with intellectual property. From the increase in patent applications swamping the government's patent office to the new laws that must be put in place to enforce copyright protection, digital technologies have impacted our behavior.

Privacy

The term *privacy* has many definitions, but for our purposes, privacy will mean the ability to control information about oneself. Our ability to maintain our privacy has eroded substantially in the past decades, due to information systems.

Personally Identifiable Information

Information about a person that can be used to uniquely establish that person's identify is called personally identifiable information, or PII. This is a broad category that includes information such as:

- name;
- social security number;
- date of birth;
- place of birth;
- mother's maiden name;
- biometric records (fingerprint, face, etc.);
- medical records;
- educational records;
- financial information; and
- employment information.

Organizations that collect PII are responsible to protect it. The Department of Commerce recommends that "organizations minimize the use, collection, and retention of PII to what is strictly necessary to accomplish their business purpose and mission." They go on to state that "the likelihood of harm caused by a breach involving PII is greatly reduced if an organization minimizes the amount of PII it uses, collects, and stores."[7] Organizations that do not protect PII can face penalties, lawsuits, and loss of business. In the US,

---

7. *Guide to Protecting the Confidentiality of Personally Identifiable Information (PII)*. National Institute of Standards and Technology, US Department of Commerce Special Publication 800-122. http://csrc.nist.gov/publications/nistpubs/800-122/sp800-122.pdf

most states now have laws in place requiring organizations that have had security breaches related to PII to notify potential victims, as does the European Union.

Just because companies are required to protect your information does not mean they are restricted from sharing it. In the US, companies can share your information without your explicit consent (see sidebar below), though not all do so. Companies that collect PII are urged by the FTC to create a privacy policy and post it on their website. The state of California requires a privacy policy for any website that does business with a resident of the state (see http://www.privacy.ca.gov/lawenforcement/laws.htm).

While the privacy laws in the US seek to balance consumer protection with promoting commerce, in the European Union privacy is considered a fundamental right that outweighs the interests of commerce. This has led to much stricter privacy protection in the EU, but also makes commerce more difficult between the US and the EU.

Non-Obvious Relationship Awareness

Digital technologies have given us many new capabilities that simplify and expedite the collection of personal information. Every time we come into contact with digital technologies, information about us is being made available. From our location to our web-surfing habits, our criminal record to our credit report, we are constantly being monitored. This information can then be aggregated to create profiles of each and every one of us. While much of the information collected was available in the past, collecting it and combining it took time and effort. Today, detailed information about us is available for purchase from different companies. Even information not categorized as PII can be aggregated in such a way that an individual can be identified.

This process of collecting large quantities of a variety of information and then combining it to create profiles of individuals is known as non-obvious relationship awareness, or NORA. First commercialized by big casinos looking to find cheaters, NORA is used by both government agencies and private organizations, and it is big business.

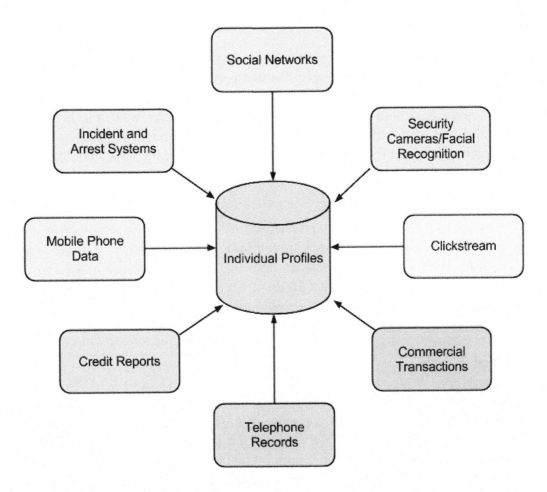

Non-obvious relationship awareness (NORA)

In some settings, NORA can bring many benefits, such as in law enforcement. By being able to identify potential criminals more quickly, crimes can be solved more quickly or even prevented before they happen. But these advantages come at a price: our privacy.

Restrictions on Record Collecting

In the US, the government has strict guidelines on how much information can be collected about its citizens. Certain classes of information have been restricted by laws over time, and the advent of digital tools has made these restrictions more important than ever.

Children's Online Privacy Protection Act

Websites that are collecting information from children under the age of thirteen are required to comply with the Children's Online Privacy Protection Act (COPPA), which is enforced by the Federal Trade Commission (FTC). To comply with COPPA, organizations must make a good-faith effort to determine the age of those accessing their websites and, if users are under thirteen years old, must obtain parental consent before collecting any information.

Family Educational Rights and Privacy Act

The Family Educational Rights and Privacy Act (FERPA) is a US law that protects the privacy of student education records. In brief, this law specifies that parents have a right to their child's educational information until the child reaches either the age of eighteen or begins attending school beyond the high school level. At that point, control of the information is given to the child. While this law is not specifically about the digital collection of information on the Internet, the educational institutions that are collecting student information are at a higher risk for disclosing it improperly because of digital technologies.

Health Insurance Portability and Accountability Act

The Health Insurance Portability and Accountability Act of 1996 (HIPAA) is the law the specifically singles out records related to health care as a special class of personally identifiable information. This law gives patients specific rights to control their medical records, requires health care providers and others who maintain this information to get specific permission in order to share it, and imposes penalties on the institutions that breach this trust. Since much of this information is now shared via electronic medical records, the protection of those systems becomes paramount.

Sidebar: Do Not Track

When it comes to getting permission to share personal information, the US and the EU have different approaches. In the US, the "opt-out" model is prevalent; in this model, the default agreement is that you have agreed to share your information with the organization and must explicitly tell them that you do not want your information shared. There are no laws prohibiting the sharing of your data (beyond some specific categories of data, such as medical records). In the European Union, the "opt-in" model is required to be the default. In this case, you must give your explicit permission before an organization can share your information.

To combat this sharing of information, the Do Not Track initiative was created. As its creators explain[8]:

> Do Not Track is a technology and policy proposal that enables users to opt out of tracking by websites they do not visit, including analytics services, advertising networks, and social platforms. At present few of these third parties offer a reliable tracking opt out, and tools for blocking them are neither user-friendly nor comprehensive. Much like the popular Do Not Call registry, Do Not Track provides users with a single, simple, persistent choice to opt out of third-party web tracking.

Summary

The rapid changes in information technology in the past few decades have brought a broad array of new capabilities and powers to governments, organizations, and individuals alike. These new capabilities have required thoughtful analysis and the creation of new norms, regulations, and laws. In this chapter, we have seen how the areas of intellectual property and privacy have been affected by these new capabilities and how the regulatory environment has been changed to address them.

8. http://donottrack.us/

Study Questions

1. What does the term *information systems ethics* mean?

2. What is a code of ethics? What is one advantage and one disadvantage of a code of ethics?

3. What does the term *intellectual property* mean? Give an example.

4. What protections are provided by a copyright? How do you obtain one?

5. What is fair use?

6. What protections are provided by a patent? How do you obtain one?

7. What does a trademark protect? How do you obtain one?

8. What does the term *personally identifiable information* mean?

9. What protections are provided by HIPAA, COPPA, and FERPA?

10. How would you explain the concept of NORA?

Exercises

1. Provide one example of how information technology has created an ethical dilemma that would not have existed before the advent of information technology.

2. Find an example of a code of ethics or acceptable use policy related to information technology and highlight five points that you think are important.

3. Do some original research on the effort to combat patent trolls. Write a two-page paper that discusses this legislation.

4. Give an example of how NORA could be used to identify an individual.

5. How are intellectual property protections different across the world? Pick two countries and do some original research, then compare the patent and copyright protections offered in those countries to those in the US. Write a two- to three-page paper describing the differences.

Chapter 13: Future Trends in Information Systems

Learning Objectives

Upon successful completion of this chapter, you will be able to:

- describe future trends in information systems.

Introduction

Information systems have evolved at a rapid pace ever since their introduction in the 1950s. Today, devices that we can hold in one hand are more powerful than the computers used to land a man on the moon. The Internet has made the entire world accessible to us, allowing us to communicate and collaborate with each other like never before. In this chapter, we will examine current trends and look ahead to what is coming next.

Global

The first trend to note is the continuing expansion of globalization. The use of the Internet is growing all over the world, and with it the use of digital devices. The growth is coming from some unexpected places; countries such as Indonesia and Iran are leading the way in Internet growth.

Country	New Internet Users (millions) 2008-2012	% Yearly Growth
China	264	10
India	88	26
Indonesia	39	58
Iran	35	205
Russia	33	6
Nigeria	31	15
Philippines	28	32
Brazil	27	6
Mexico	19	9
USA	18	3

Data source: internetworldstats.com

Global Internet growth, 2008–2012. Click to enlarge.
(Source: Internet World Stats)

Social

Social media growth is another trend that continues. Facebook now has over one billion users! In 2013, 80% of Facebook users were outside of the US and Canada.[1] Countries where Facebook is growing rapidly include Indonesia, Mexico, and the Philippines. [2]

Besides Facebook, other social media sites are also seeing tremendous growth. Over 70% of YouTube's users are outside the US, with the UK, India, Germany, Canada, France, South Korea, and Russia leading the way.[3] Pinterest gets over 50% of its users from outside the US, with over 9% from India. [4] Twitter now has over 230 million active users. [5] Social media sites not based in the US are also growing. China's QQ instant-messaging service is the eighth most-visited site in the world.[6]

Personal

Ever since the advent of Web 2.0 and e-commerce, users of information systems have expected to be able to modify their experiences to meet their personal tastes. From custom backgrounds on computer desktops to unique ringtones on mobile phones, makers of digital devices provide the ability to personalize how we use them. More recently, companies such as Netflix have begun assisting their users with personalizations by making suggestions. In the future, we will begin seeing devices perfectly matched to our personal preferences, based upon information collected about us in the past.

Mobile

Perhaps the most impactful trend in digital technologies in the last decade has been the advent of mobile technologies. Beginning with the simple cellphone in the 1990s and evolving into the smartphones and tablets of today, the growth of mobile has been overwhelming. Here are some key indicators of this trend:

- Mobile device sales. In 2011, smartphones began outselling personal computers.[7]
- The number of smartphone subscribers grew at 31% in 2013, with China leading the way at 354 million smartphone users.
- Internet access via mobile. In May of 2013, mobile accounted for 15% of all Internet traffic. In China, 75% of Internet users used their smartphone to access it. Facebook reported that 68% of its active users used their mobile platform to access the social network.
- The rise of tablets. While Apple defined the smartphone with the iPhone, the iPad sold more than three times as many units in its first twelve months as the iPhone did in its first twelve months. Tablet shipments now outpace notebook PCs and desktop PCs. The research firm IDC predicts that 87% of all connected devices will be either smartphones or tablets by 2017. [8]

1. http://newsroom.fb.com/Key-Facts
2. http://www.socialbakers.com/blog/38-top-10-countries-on-facebook-in-the-last-six-months
3. http://newmediarockstars.com/2013/03/the-top-10-countries-in-youtube-viewership-outside-the-usa-infographic/
4. http://www.alexa.com/siteinfo/pinterest.com
5. https://about.twitter.com/company
6. http://www.alexa.com/siteinfo/qq.com
7. http://mashable.com/2012/02/03/smartphone-sales-overtake-pcs/

Wearable

The average smartphone user looks at his or her smartphone 150 times a day for functions such as messaging (23 times), phone calls (22), listening to music (13), and social media (9).[9] Many of these functions would be much better served if the technology was worn on, or even physically integrated into, our bodies. This technology is known as a "wearable."

Google Glass. Click to enlarge. (CC-BY: Flickr, user Tedeytan)

Wearables have been around for a long time, with technologies such as hearing aids and, later, bluetooth earpieces. But now, we are seeing an explosion of new wearable technologies. Perhaps the best known of these is Google Glass, an augmented reality device that you wear over your eyes like a pair of eyeglasses. Visible only to you, Google Glass will project images into your field of vision based on your context and voice commands. You can find out much more about Google Glass at http://www.google.com/glass/start/.

Another class of wearables are those related to health care. The UP by Jawbone consists of a wristband and an app that tracks how you sleep, move, and eat, then helps you use that information to feel your best. [10] It can be used to track your sleep patterns, moods, eating patterns, and other aspects of daily life, and then report back to you via an app on your smartphone or tablet. As our population ages and technology continues to evolve, there will be a large increase in wearables like this.

Collaborative

As more of us use smartphones and wearables, it will be simpler than ever to share data with each other for mutual benefit. Some of this sharing can be done passively, such as reporting our location in order to update traffic statistics. Other data can be reported actively, such as adding our rating of a restaurant to a review site.

The smartphone app Waze is a community-based tool that keeps track of the route you are traveling and how fast you are making your way to your destination. In return for providing your data, you can benefit from the data being sent from all of the other users of the app. Waze will route you around traffic and accidents based upon real-time reports from other users.

Yelp! allows consumers to post ratings and reviews of local businesses into a database, and then it provides that data back to consumers via its website or mobile phone app. By compiling ratings of restaurants, shopping centers, and services, and then allowing consumers to search through its directory, Yelp! has become a huge source of business for many companies. Unlike data collected passively however, Yelp! relies on its users to take the time to provide honest ratings and reviews.

8. http://www.forbes.com/sites/louiscolumbus/2013/09/12/idc-87-of-connected-devices-by-2017-will-be-tablets-and-smartphones/

9. http://communities-dominate.blogs.com/brands/2013/03/the-annual-mobile-industry-numbers-and-stats-blog-yep-this-year-we-will-hit-the-mobile-moment.html

10. https://jawbone.com/up

Printable

One of the most amazing innovations to be developed recently is the 3-D printer. A 3-D printer allows you to print virtually any 3-D object based on a model of that object designed on a computer. 3-D printers work by creating layer upon layer of the model using malleable materials, such as different types of glass, metals, or even wax.

3-D printing is quite useful for prototyping the designs of products to determine their feasibility and marketability. 3-D printing has also been used to create working prosthetic legs, handguns, and even an ear that can hear beyond the range of normal hearing. The US Air Force now uses 3-D printed parts on the F-18 fighter jet.[11]

3-D printing is one of many technologies embraced by the "maker" movement. Chris Anderson, editor of *Wired* magazine, puts it this way[12]:

> In a nutshell, the term "Maker" refers to a new category of builders who are using open-source methods and the latest technology to bring manufacturing out of its traditional factory context, and into the realm of the personal desktop computer. Until recently, the ability to manufacture was reserved for those who owned factories. What's happened over the last five years is that we've brought the Web's democratizing power to manufacturing. Today, you can manufacture with the push of a button.

Findable

The "Internet of Things" refers to the idea of physical objects being connected to the Internet. Advances in wireless technologies and sensors will allow physical objects to send and receive data about themselves. Many of the technologies to enable this are already available – it is just a matter of integrating them together.

In a 2010 report by McKinsey & Company on the Internet of Things[13], six broad applications are identified:

- Tracking behavior. When products are embedded with sensors, companies can track the movements of these products and even monitor interactions with them. Business models can be fine-tuned to take advantage of this behavioral data. Some insurance companies, for example, are offering to install location sensors in customers' cars. That allows these companies to base the price of policies on how a car is driven as well as where it travels.

- Enhanced situational awareness. Data from large numbers of sensors deployed, for example, in infrastructure (such as roads and buildings), or to report on environmental conditions (including soil moisture, ocean currents, or weather), can give decision makers a heightened awareness of real-time events, particularly when the sensors are used with advanced display or visualization technologies. Security personnel, for instance, can use sensor networks that combine video, audio, and vibration detectors to spot unauthorized individuals who enter restricted areas.

11. http://www.economist.com/news/technology-quarterly/21584447-digital-manufacturing-there-lot-hype-around-3d-printing-it-fast

12. Makers: The New Industrial Revolution by Chris Anderson. Crown Business; 2012.

13. http://www.mckinsey.com/insights/high_tech_telecoms_internet/the_internet_of_things

- Sensor-driven decision analysis. The Internet of Things also can support longer-range, more complex human planning and decision making. The technology requirements – tremendous storage and computing resources linked with advanced software systems that generate a variety of graphical displays for analyzing data – rise accordingly.

- Process optimization. Some industries, such as chemical production, are installing legions of sensors to bring much greater granularity to monitoring. These sensors feed data to computers, which in turn analyze the data and then send signals to actuators that adjust processes – for example, by modifying ingredient mixtures, temperatures, or pressures.

- Optimized resource consumption. Networked sensors and automated feedback mechanisms can change usage patterns for scarce resources, such as energy and water. This can be accomplished by dynamically changing the price of these goods to increase or reduce demand.

- Complex autonomous systems. The most demanding use of the Internet of Things involves the rapid, real-time sensing of unpredictable conditions and instantaneous responses guided by automated systems. This kind of machine decision-making mimics human reactions, though at vastly enhanced performance levels. The automobile industry, for instance, is stepping up the development of systems that can detect imminent collisions and take evasive action.

Autonomous

A final trend that is emerging is an extension of the Internet of Things: autonomous robots and vehicles. By combining software, sensors, and location technologies, devices that can operate themselves to perform specific functions are being developed. These take the form of creations such as medical nanotechnology robots (nanobots), self-driving cars, or unmanned aerial vehicles (UAVs).

A nanobot is a robot whose components are on the scale of about a nanometer, which is one-billionth of a meter. While still an emerging field, it is showing promise for applications in the medical field. For example, a set of nanobots could be introduced into the human body to combat cancer or a specific disease.

In March of 2012, Google introduced the world to their driverless car by releasing a video on YouTube showing a blind man driving the car around the San Francisco area. The car combines several technologies, including a laser radar system, worth about $150,000. While the car is not available commercially yet, three US states (Nevada, Florida, and California) have already passed legislation making driverless cars legal.

A UAV, often referred to as a "drone," is a small airplane or helicopter that can fly without a pilot. Instead of a pilot, they are either run autonomously by computers in the vehicle or operated by a person using a remote control. While most drones today are used for military or civil applications, there is a growing market for personal drones. For around $300, a consumer can purchase a drone for personal use.

Summary

As the world of information technology moves forward, we will be constantly challenged by new capabilities and innovations that will both amaze and disgust us. As we learned in chapter 12, many times the new capabilities and powers that come with these new technologies will test us and require a new way of thinking about the world. Businesses and individuals alike need to be aware of these coming changes and prepare for them.

Study Questions

1. Which countries are the biggest users of the Internet? Social media? Mobile?

2. Which country had the largest Internet growth (in %) between 2008 and 2012?

3. How will most people connect to the Internet in the future?

4. What are two different applications of wearable technologies?

5. What are two different applications of collaborative technologies?

6. What capabilities do printable technologies have?

7. How will advances in wireless technologies and sensors make objects "findable"?

8. What is enhanced situational awareness?

9. What is a nanobot?

10. What is a UAV?

Exercises

1. If you were going to start a new technology business, which of the emerging trends do you think would be the biggest opportunity? Do some original research to estimate the market size.

2. What privacy concerns could be raised by collaborative technologies such as Waze?

3. Do some research about the first handgun printed using a 3-D printer and report on some of the concerns raised.

4. Write up an example of how the Internet of Things might provide a business with a competitive advantage.

5. How do you think wearable technologies could improve overall healthcare?

6. What potential problems do you see with a rise in the number of driverless cars? Do some independent research and write a two-page paper that describes where driverless cars are legal and what problems may occur.

7. Seek out the latest presentation by Mary Meeker on "Internet Trends" (if you cannot find it, the video from 2013 is available at http://allthingsd.com/20130529/mary-meekers-2013-internet-trends-deck-the-full-video/). Write a one-page paper describing what the top three trends are, in your opinion.

Answers to Study Questions

Chapter 1

1. What are the five components that make up an information system?
   a. *hardware, software, data, people, process*
2. What are three examples of information system hardware?
   a. *There are a number of possible answers: a PC, a printer, a mouse, tablets, mobile phones, etc.*
3. Microsoft Windows is an example of which component of information systems?
   a. *It is an operating system, which is a part of the software component.*
4. What is application software?
   a. *Software that does something useful.*
5. What roles do people play in information systems?
   a. *The text includes examples such as helpdesk support, systems analyst, programmer, and CIO.*
6. What is the definition of a process?
   a. *A process is a series of steps undertaken to achieve a desired outcome or goal.*
7. What was invented first, the personal computer or the Internet (ARPANET)?
   a. *The Internet was activated in 1969; the personal computer was introduced in 1975.*
8. In what year were restrictions on commercial use of the Internet first lifted? When were eBay and Amazon founded?
   a. *Restrictions were lifted in 1991, Amazon was founded in 1994, and eBay was founded in 1995.*
9. What does it mean to say we are in a "post-PC world"?
   a. *The personal computer will no longer be the primary way that people interact and do business.*
10. What is Carr's main argument about information technology?
    a. *That information technology is just a commodity and cannot be used to gain a competitive advantage.*

Chapter 2

1. Write your own description of what the term *information systems hardware* means.
   a. *Answers will vary, but should say something about information systems hardware consisting of the physical parts of computing devices that can actually be touched.*
2. What is the impact of Moore's Law on the various hardware components described in this chapter?
   a. *The student should pick one of the components and discuss the impact of the fact that computing doubles in speed every two years. Most devices are getting smaller, faster, cheaper, and this should be indicated in the answer.*
3. Write a summary of one of the items linked to in the "Integrated Computing" section.
   a. *The student should write a summary of one of the linked articles.*

4. Explain why the personal computer is now considered a commodity.

  a. The PC has become a commodity in the sense that there is very little differentiation between computers, and the primary factor that controls their sale is their price.

5. The CPU can also be thought of as the _____ of the computer.

  a. brain

6. List the following in increasing order (slowest to fastest): megahertz, kilohertz, gigahertz.

  a. kilohertz, megahertz, gigahertz

7. What is the bus of a computer?

  a. The bus is the electrical connection between different computer components.

8. Name two differences between RAM and a hard disk.

  a. RAM is volatile; the hard disk is non-volatile. Data access in RAM is faster than on the hard disk.

9. What are the advantages of solid-state drives over hard disks?

  a. The main advantage is speed: an SSD has much faster data-access speeds than a traditional hard disk.

10. How heavy was the first commercially successful portable computer?

  a. The Compaq PC was 28 pounds.

Chapter 3

1. Come up with your own definition of software. Explain the key terms in your definition.

  a. A variety of answers are possible, but should be similar to the definition in the text: Software is the set of instructions that tell the hardware what to do. Software is created through the process of programming.

2. What are the functions of the operating system?

  a. The operating system manages the hardware resources of the computer, provides the user-interface components, and provides a platform for software developers to write applications.

3. Which of the following are operating systems and which are applications: Microsoft Excel, Google Chrome, iTunes, Windows, Android, Angry Birds.

  a. Microsoft Excel (application), Google Chrome (application), iTunes (application), WIndows (operating system), Android (operating system), Angry Birds (application)

4. What is your favorite software application? What tasks does it help you accomplish?

  a. Students will have various answers to this question. They should pick an application, not an operating system. They should be able to list at least one thing that it helps them accomplish.

5. What is a "killer" app? What was the killer app for the PC?

  a. A killer app is application software that is so useful that people will purchase the hardware just so they can run it. The killer app for the PC was the spreadsheet (Visicalc).

6. How would you categorize the software that runs on mobile devices? Break down these apps into at least three basic categories and give an example of each.

  a. There are various ways to answer this question. Students should identify that there are mobile operating systems and mobile apps. Most likely, students will break down mobile apps into multiple categories: games, GPS, reading, communication, etc.

7. Explain what an ERP system does.

  a. An ERP (enterprise resource planning) system is a software application with a centralized database that is implemented across the entire organization.

8. What is open-source software? How does it differ from closed-source software? Give an example of each.

a. Open-source software is software that makes the source code available for anyone to copy and use. It is free to download, copy, and distribute. Closed-source software does not make the source code available and generally is not free to download, copy, and distribute. There are many examples of both, such as: Firefox (open source), Linux (open source), iTunes (closed source), Microsoft Office (closed source).

9. What does a software license grant?

a. Software licenses are not all the same, but generally they grant the user the right to use the software on a limited basis. The terms of the license dictate users' rights in detail.

10. How did the Y2K (year 2000) problem affect the sales of ERP systems?

a. Organizations purchased ERP software to replace their older systems in order to avoid any problems with the year 2000 in their software.

Chapter 4

1. What is the difference between data, information, and knowledge?

a. Data are the raw bits and pieces of facts and statistics with no context. Data can be quantitative or qualitative. Information is data that has been given context. Knowledge is information that has been aggregated and analyzed and can be used for making decisions.

2. Explain in your own words how the data component relates to the hardware and software components of information systems.

a. There are numerous answers to this question, but all should be variations on the following: Data is processed by the hardware via software. A database is software that runs on the hardware. Hardware stores the data, software processes the data.

3. What is the difference between quantitative data and qualitative data? In what situations could the number 42 be considered qualitative data?

a. Quantitative data is numeric, the result of a measurement, count, or some other mathematical calculation. Qualitative data is descriptive. The number 42 could be qualitative if it is a designation instead of a measurement, count, or calculation. For example: that player's jersey has number 42 on it.

4. What are the characteristics of a relational database?

a. A relational database is one in which data is organized into one or more tables. Each table has a set of fields, which define the nature of the data stored in the table. A record is one instance of a set of fields in a table. All the tables are related by one or more fields in common.

5. When would using a personal DBMS make sense?

a. When working on a smaller database for personal use, or when disconnected from the network.

6. What is the difference between a spreadsheet and a database? List three differences between them.

a. A database is generally more powerful and complex than a spreadsheet, with the ability to handle multiple types of data and link them together. Some differences: A database has defined field types, a spreadsheet does not. A database uses a standardized query language (such as SQL), a spreadsheet does not. A database can hold much larger amounts of data than a spreadsheet.

7. Describe what the term *normalization* means.

a. To normalize a database means to design it in a way that: 1) reduces duplication of data between tables and 2) gives the table as much flexibility as possible.

8. Why is it important to define the data type of a field when designing a relational database?

a. A data type tells the database what functions can be performed with the data. The second important reason to define the data type is so that the proper amount of storage space is allocated for the data.

9. Name a database you interact with frequently. What would some of the field names be?

a. The student can choose any sort of system that they interact with, such as Amazon or their school's online systems. The fields would be the names of data being collected, such as "first name", or "address".

10. What is metadata?

a. Metadata is data about data. It refers to the data used to describe other data, such as the length of a song in iTunes, which describes the music file.

11. Name three advantages of using a data warehouse.

a. The text lists the following (the student should pick at least three of these):

i. The process of developing a data warehouse forces an organization to better understand the data that it is currently collecting and, equally important, what data is not being collected.

ii. A data warehouse provides a centralized view of all data being collected across the enterprise and provides a means of determining data that is inconsistent.

iii. Once all data is identified as consistent, an organization can generate one version of the truth. This is important when the company wants to report consistent statistics about itself, such as revenue or number of employees.

iv. By having a data warehouse, snapshots of data can be taken over time. This creates a historical record of data, which allows for an analysis of trends.

v. A data warehouse provides tools to combine data, which can provide new information and analysis.

12. What is data mining?

a. Data mining is the process of analyzing data to find previously unknown trends, patterns, and associations in order to make decisions.

Chapter 5

1. What were the first four locations hooked up to the Internet (ARPANET)?

a. UCLA, Stanford, MIT, and the University of Utah

2. What does the term *packet* mean?

a. The fundamental unit of data transmitted over the Internet. Each packet has the sender's address, the destination address, a sequence number, and a piece of the overall message to be sent.

3. Which came first, the Internet or the World Wide Web?

a. the Internet

4. What was revolutionary about Web 2.0?

a. Anyone could post content to the web, without the need for understanding HTML or web-server technology.

5. What was the so-called killer app for the Internet?

a. electronic mail (e-mail)

6. What makes a connection a *broadband* connection?

a. A broadband connection is defined as one that has speeds of at least 256,000 bps.

7. What does the term VoIP mean?

a. Voice over Internet protocol – a way to have voice conversations over the Internet.

8. What is an LAN?

a. An LAN is a local network, usually operating in the same building or on the same campus.

9. What is the difference between an intranet and an extranet?

a. An intranet consists of the set of web pages and resources available on a company's internal network. These items are not available to those outside of the company. An extranet is a part of the company's network that is made available securely to those outside of the company. Extranets can be used to allow customers to log in and check the status of their orders, or for suppliers to check their customers' inventory levels.

10. What is Metcalfe's Law?

a. Metcalfe's Law states that the value of a telecommunications network is proportional to the square of the number of connected users of the system.

Chapter 6

1. Briefly define each of the three members of the information security triad.

a. The three members are as follows:

i. Confidentiality: we want to be able to restrict access to those who are allowed to see given information.

ii. Integrity: the assurance that the information being accessed has not been altered and truly represents what is intended.

iii. Availability: information can be accessed and modified by anyone authorized to do so in an appropriate timeframe.

2. What does the term *authentication* mean?

a. The process of ensuring that a person is who he or she claims to be.

3. What is multi-factor authentication?

a. The use of more than one method of authentication. The methods are: something you know, something you have, and something you are.

4. What is role-based access control?

a. With role-based access control (RBAC), instead of giving specific users access rights to an information resource, users are assigned to roles and then those roles are assigned the access.

5. What is the purpose of encryption?

a. To keep transmitted data secret so that only those with the proper key can read it.

6. What are two good examples of a complex password?

a. There are many examples of this. Students need to provide examples of passwords that are a minimum of eight characters, with at least one upper-case letter, one special character, and one number.

7. What is pretexting?

a. Pretexting occurs when an attacker calls a helpdesk or security administrator and pretends to be a particular authorized user having trouble logging in. Then, by providing some personal information about the authorized user, the attacker convinces the security person to reset the password and tell him what it is.

8. What are the components of a good backup plan?

a. Knowing what needs to be backed up, regular backups of all data, offsite storage of all backed-up data, and a test of the restoration process.

9. What is a firewall?

a. A firewall can be either a hardware firewall or a software firewall. A hardware firewall is a device that is connected to the network and filters the packets based on a set of rules. A software firewall runs on the operating system and intercepts packets as they arrive to a computer.

10. What does the term *physical security* mean?

a. Physical security is the protection of the actual hardware and networking components that store and transmit information resources.

Chapter 7

1. What is the productivity paradox?

a. The productivity paradox is based on Erik Brynjolfsson's finding, based on research he conducted in the early 1990s, that the addition of information technology to business had not improved productivity at all.

2. Summarize Carr's argument in "Does IT Matter."

a. Information technology is now a commodity and cannot be used to provide an organization with competitive advantage.

3. How is the 2008 study by Brynjolfsson and McAfee different from previous studies? How is it the same?

a. It is different because it shows that IT can bring a competitive advantage, given the right conditions. It is the same in the sense that it shows that IT, by itself, does not bring competitive advantage.

4. What does it mean for a business to have a competitive advantage?

a. A company is said to have a competitive advantage over its rivals when it is able to sustain profits that exceed average for the industry.

5. What are the primary activities and support activities of the value chain?

a. The primary activities are those that directly impact the creation of a product or service. The support activities are those that support the primary activities. Primary: inbound logistics, operations, outbound logistics, sales/marketing, and service. Support: firm infrastructure, human resources, technology development, and procurement.

6. What has been the overall impact of the Internet on industry profitability? Who has been the true winner?

a. The overall impact has been a reduction in average industry profitability. The consumer has been the true winner.

7. How does EDI work?

a. EDI is the computer-to-computer exchange of business documents in a standard electronic format between business partners.

8. Give an example of a semi-structured decision and explain what inputs would be necessary to provide assistance in making the decision.

a. A semi-structured decision is one in which most of the factors needed for making the decision are known but human experience and other outside factors may still play a role. The student should provide an example of a decision that uses an information system to provide information but is not made by the system. Examples would include: budgeting decisions, diagnosing a medical condition, and investment decisions.

9. What does a collaborative information system do?

a. A collaborative system is software that allows multiple users to interact on a document or topic in order to complete a task or make a decision.

10. How can IT play a role in competitive advantage, according to the 2008 article by Brynjolfsson and McAfee?

a. The article suggests that IT can influence competitive advantage when good management develops and delivers IT-supported process innovation.

Chapter 8

1. What does the term *business process* mean?

a. A process is a series of tasks that are completed in order to accomplish a goal. A business process, therefore, is a process that is focused on achieving a goal for a business.

2. What are three examples of business process from a job you have had or an organization you have observed?

a. Students can answer this in almost any way. The examples should consist of more than a single step.

3. What is the value in documenting a business process?

a. There are many answers to this. From the text: it allows for better control of the process, and for standardization.

4. What is an ERP system? How does an ERP system enforce best practices for an organization?

a. An ERP (enterprise resource planning) system is a software application with a centralized database that is implemented across the entire organization. It enforces best practices through the business processes embedded in the software.

5. What is one of the criticisms of ERP systems?

a. ERP systems can lead to the commoditization of business processes, meaning that every company that uses an ERP system will perform business processes the same way.

6. What is business process reengineering? How is it different from incrementally improving a process?

a. Business process reengineering (BPR) occurs when a business process is redesigned from the ground up. It is different from incrementally improving a process in that it does not simply take the existing process and modify it.

7. Why did BPR get a bad name?

a. BPR became an excuse to lay off employees and try to complete the same amount of work using fewer employees.

8. List the guidelines for redesigning a business process.

a. The guidelines are as follows:

i. Organize around outcomes, not tasks.

ii. Have those who use the outcomes of the process perform the process.

iii. Subsume information-processing work into the real work that produces the information. Treat geographically dispersed resources as though they were centralized.

iv. Link parallel activities instead of integrating their results.

v. Put the decision points where the work is performed, and build controls into the process.

vi. Capture information once, at the source.

9. What is business process management? What role does it play in allowing a company to differentiate itself?

a. Business process management (BPM) can be thought of as an intentional effort to plan, document, implement, and distribute an organization's business processes with the support of information technology. It can play a role in differentiation through built-in reporting, and by empowering employees, enforcing best practices, and enforcing consistency.

10. What does ISO certification signify?

a. ISO certification shows that you know what you do, do what you say, and have documented your processes.

Chapter 9

1. Describe the role of a systems analyst.

a. To understand business requirements and translate them into the requirements of an information system.

2. What are some of the different roles for a computer engineer?

a. hardware engineer, software engineer, network engineer, systems engineer

3. What are the duties of a computer operator?

a. Duties include keeping the operating systems up to date, ensuring available memory and disk storage, and overseeing the physical environment of the computer.

4. What does the CIO do?

a. The CIO aligns the plans and operations of the information systems with the strategic goals of the organization. This includes tasks such as budgeting, strategic planning, and personnel decisions relevant to the information-systems function.

5. Describe the job of a project manager.

a. A project manager is responsible for keeping projects on time and on budget. This person works with the stakeholders of the project to keep the team organized and communicates the status of the project to management.

6. Explain the point of having two different career paths in information systems.

a. To allow for career growth for those who do not want to manage other employees but instead want to focus on technical skills.

7. What are the advantages and disadvantages of centralizing the IT function?

a. There are several possible answers here. Advantages of centralizing include more control over the company's systems and data. Disadvantages include a more limited availability of IT resources.

8. What impact has information technology had on the way companies are organized?

a. The organizational structure has been flattened, with fewer layers of management.

9. What are the five types of information-systems users?

a. innovators, early adopters, early majority, late majority, laggards

10. Why would an organization outsource?

a. Because it needs a specific skill for a limited amount of time, and/or because it can cut costs by outsourcing.

Chapter 10

1. What are the steps in the SDLC methodology?

a. The steps are Preliminary Analysis, System Analysis, System Design, Programming, Testing, Implementation, and Maintenance.

2. What is RAD software development?

a. Rapid application development (RAD) is a software-development (or systems-development) methodology that focuses on quickly building a working model of the software, getting feedback from users, and then using that feedback to update the working model.

3. What makes the lean methodology unique?

a. The biggest difference between the lean methodology and the other methodologies is that the full set of requirements for the system is not known when the project is launched.

4. What are three differences between second-generation and third-generation languages?

a. Three key differences are as follows:

i. The words used in the language: third generation languages use more English-like words than second-generation languages.

ii. Hardware specificity: third generation languages are not specific to hardware, second-generation languages are.

iii. Learning curve: third generation languages are easier to learn and use.

5. Why would an organization consider building its own software application if it is cheaper to buy one?

a. They may wish to build their own in order to have something that is unique (different from their competitors), and/or something that more closely matches their business processes. They also may choose to do this if they have more time and/or more money available to do it.

6. What is responsive design?

a. Responsive design is a method of developing websites that allows them to be viewed on many different types of devices without losing capability or effectiveness. With a responsive website, images resize themselves based on the size of the device's screen, and text flows and sizes itself properly for optimal viewing.

7. What is the relationship between HTML and CSS in website design?

a. While HTML is used to define the components of a web page, cascading style sheets (CSS) are used to define the styles of the components on a page.

8. What is the difference between the pilot implementation methodology and the parallel implementation methodology?

a. The pilot methodology implements new software for just one group of people while the rest of the users use the previous version of the software. The parallel implementation methodology uses both the old and the new applications at the same time.

9. What is change management?

a. The oversight of the changes brought about in an organization.

10. What are the four different implementation methodologies?

a. direct cutover, pilot, parallel, phased

Chapter 11

1. What does the term *globalization* mean?

a. Globalization *refers to the integration of goods, services, and cultures among the nations of the world.*

2. How does Friedman define the three eras of globalization?

a. The three eras are as follows:

i. "Globalization 1.0" occurred from 1492 until about 1800. In this era, globalization was centered around countries. It was about how much horsepower, wind power, and steam power a country had and how creatively it was deployed. The world shrank from size "large" to size "medium."

      ii. "Globalization 2.0" occurred from about 1800 until 2000, interrupted only by the two World Wars. In this era, the dynamic force driving change was comprised of multinational companies. The world shrank from size "medium" to size "small."

      iii. "Globalization 3.0" is our current era, beginning in the year 2000. The convergence of the personal computer, fiber-optic Internet connections, and software has created a "flat-world platform" that allows small groups and even individuals to go global. The world has shrunk from size "small" to size "tiny."

3. Which technologies have had the biggest effect on globalization?

      a. There are several answers to this. Probably the most obvious are the Internet, the graphical interface of Windows and the World Wide Web, and workflow software.

4. What are some of the advantages brought about by globalization?

      a. Advantages include the ability to locate expertise and labor around the world, the ability to operate 24 hours a day, and a larger market for products.

5. What are the challenges of globalization?

      a. Challenges include infrastructure differences, labor laws and regulations, legal restrictions, and different languages, customs, and preferences.

6. What does the term *digital divide* mean?

      a. The separation between those who have access to the global network and those who do not. The digital divide can occur between countries, regions, or even neighborhoods.

7. What are Jakob Nielsen's three stages of the digital divide?

      a. economic, usability, and empowerment

8. What was one of the key points of *The Rise of the Network Society*?

      a. There are two key points to choose from. One is that economic activity was, when the book was published in 1996, being organized around the networks that the new telecommunication technologies had provided. The other is that this new, global economic activity was different from the past, because "it is an economy with the capacity to work as a unit in real time on a planetary scale."

9. Which country has the highest average Internet speed? How does your country compare?

      a. According to the chart in the chapter, South Korea has the highest Internet speeds. Students will need to look up their own to compare.

10. What is the OLPC project? Has it been successful?

      a. One Laptop Per Child. By most measures, it has not been a successful program.

Chapter 12

1. What does the term *information systems ethics* mean?

      a. There are various ways of answering this question, but the answer should include something about the application of ethics to the new capabilities and cultural norms brought about by information technology.

2. What is a code of ethics? What is one advantage and one disadvantage of a code of ethics?

      a. A code of ethics is a document that outlines a set of acceptable behaviors for a professional or social group. Answers may differ for the second part, but from the text: one advantage of a code of ethics is that it clarifies the acceptable standards of behavior for a professional group. One disadvantage is that it does not necessarily have legal authority.

3. What does the term *intellectual property* mean? Give an example.

      a. Intellectual property is defined as "property (as an idea, invention, or process) that derives from the work of the mind or intellect."

4. What protections are provided by a copyright? How do you obtain one?

   a. Copyright protections address the following: who can make copies of the work, who can make derivative works from the original work, who can perform the work publicly, who can display the work publicly, and who can distribute the work. You obtain a copyright as soon as the work is put into tangible form.

5. What is fair use?

   a. Fair use is a limitation on copyright law that allows for the use of protected works without prior authorization in specific cases.

6. What protections are provided by a patent? How do you obtain one?

   a. Once a patent is granted, it provides the inventor with protection from others infringing on the patent. In the US, a patent holder has the right to "exclude others from making, using, offering for sale, or selling the invention throughout the United States or importing the invention into the United States for a limited time in exchange for public disclosure of the invention when the patent is granted." You obtain a patent by filing an application with the patent office. A patent will be granted if the work is deemed to be original, useful, and non-obvious.

7. What does a trademark protect? How do you obtain one?

   a. A trademark protects a word, phrase, logo, shape, or sound that identifies a source of goods or services. You can obtain one by registering with the Patent and Trademark Office (US). There is also a common-law trademark.

8. What does the term *personally identifiable information* mean?

   a. Information about a person that can be used to uniquely establish that person's identity is called personally identifiable information, or PII.

9. What protections are provided by HIPAA, COPPA, and FERPA?

   a. The answers are as follows:

   i. HIPAA: protects records related to health care as a special class of personally identifiable information.

   ii. COPPA: protects information collected from children under the age of thirteen.

   iii. FERPA: protects student educational records.

10. How would you explain the concept of NORA?

    a. There are various ways to answer this. The basic answer is that NORA (non-obvious relationship awareness) is the process of collecting large quantities of a variety of information and then combining it to create profiles of individuals.

Chapter 13

1. Which countries are the biggest users of the Internet? Social media? Mobile?

   a. Students will need to look outside the text for this, as it changes all the time. There are also different ways of measurement: number of users, % of population, most active users, etc. Some good sites to use are Internet World Stats, Kissmetrics, and the World Bank.

2. Which country had the largest Internet growth (in %) between 2008 and 2012?

   a. Iran, at 205%

3. How will most people connect to the Internet in the future?

   a. via mobile devices

4. What are two different applications of wearable technologies?

   a. There are many answers to this question; two examples are Google Glass and Jawbone UP.

5. What are two different applications of collaborative technologies?

a. There are many answers to this; two examples are software that routes us to our destination in the shortest amount of time, and websites that review different companies.

6. What capabilities do printable technologies have?

a. Using 3-D printers, designers can quickly test prototypes or build something as a proof of concept. Printable technologies also make it possible to bring manufacturing to the desktop computer.

7. How will advances in wireless technologies and sensors make objects "findable"?

a. Advances in wireless technologies and sensors will allow physical objects to send and receive data about themselves.

8. What is enhanced situational awareness?

a. Data from large numbers of sensors can give decision makers a heightened awareness of real-time events, particularly when the sensors are used with advanced display or visualization technologies.

9. What is a nanobot?

a. A nanobot is a robot whose components are on the scale of about a nanometer.

10. What is a UAV?

a. An unmanned aerial vehicle – a small airplane or helicopter that can fly without a pilot. UAVs are run by computer or remote control.

Anderson, Chris. *Makers: The New Industrial Revolution*. New York: Crown Business, 2012.

Brynjolfsson, Erik. "The Productivity Paradox of Information Technology: Review and Assessment." *Communications of the ACM*, December, 1993. http://ccs.mit.edu/papers/CCSWP130/ccswp130.html.

Brynjolfsson, Erik and Lorin Hitt. "Beyond the Productivity Paradox: Computers are the Catalyst for Bigger Changes." *Communications of the ACM*, August 1998, vol. 41(8): pp. 49–55. http://ebusiness.mit.edu/erik/bpp.pdf

Castells, Manuel. *The Rise of the Network Society*. 2nd ed. Cambridge, MA: Blackwell Publishers, 2000.Valacich, Joseph, and Christoph Schneider. *Information Systems Today: Managing in the Digital World*. 4th ed. Upper Saddle River, NJ: Prentice-Hall, 2010.

Chui, Michael, Markus Löffler, and Roger Roberts. "The Internet of Things." *McKinsey Quarterly*, March 2010. http://www.mckinsey.com/insights/high_tech_telecoms_internet/the_internet_of_things

Columbus, Louis. "IDC: 87% of Connected Devices Sales by 2017 Will Be Tablets and Smartphones." Tech section of forbes.com, September 12, 2013. http://www.forbes.com/sites/louiscolumbus/2013/09/12/idc-87-of-connected-devices-by-2017-will-be-tablets-and-smartphones/

Friedman, T. L. *The World Is Flat: A Brief History of the Twenty-First Century*. New York: Farrar, Straus and Giroux, 2005.

Gallagher, Sean. "Born to Be Breached: The Worst Passwords Are Still the Most Common." *Arstechnica*, November 3, 2012. Retrieved from http://arstechnica.com/information-technology/2012/11/born-to-be-breached-the-worst-passwords-are-still-the-most-common/ on May 15, 2013.

Godin, Seth. *Really Bad PowerPoint (and How to Avoid It)*. Do You Zoom, Inc., 2001. http://www.sethgodin.com/freeprize/reallybad-1.pdf.

Guel, Michele D. "A Short Primer for Developing Security Policies." SANS Institute, 2007. Accessed from http://www.sans.org/security-resources/policies/Policy_Primer.pdf on May 31, 2013.

Hammer, Michael. "Reengineering Work: Don't Automate, Obliterate." *Harvard Business* Review, 68.4 (1990): 104–112.

Kibum, Kim. "Challenges in HCI: Digital Divide." *Crossroads*, vol. 12, issue 2 (December 2005), 2–2, doi: 10.1145/1144375.1144377. http://doi.acm.org/10.1145/1144375.1144377.

Kim, P., E. Buckner, T. Makany, and H. Kim. "A Comparative Analysis of a Game-Based Mobile Learning Model in Low-Socioeconomic Communities of India." *International Journal of Educational Development*, vol. 32, issue 2 (March 2012), pp. 205–366, doi:10.1016/j.ijedudev.2011.05.008.

Kraemer, Kenneth L., Jason Dedrick, and Prakul Sharma. "One Laptop Per Child: Vision vs. Reality." *Communications of the ACM*, vol. 52, no. 6, pp. 66–73.

Laudon, Kenneth C., and Jane P. Laudon. *Management Information Systems: Managing the Digital Firm*. 12th ed. Upper Saddle River, NJ: Prentice-Hall, 2012.

McAfee, Andrew and Erik Brynjolfsson. "Investing in the IT That Makes a Competitive Difference." *Harvard Business Review*, July-August, 2008.

McCallister, Erika, Tim Grance, and Karen Scarfone. *Guide to Protecting the Confidentiality of Personally Identifiable Information (PII)*. National Institute of Standards and Technology, US Department of Commerce Special Publication 800-122, April 2010. http://csrc.nist.gov/publications/nistpubs/800-122/sp800-122.pdf

Moore, Gordon E. "Cramming More Components onto Integrated Circuits." *Electronics*, pp. 114–117, April 19, 1965.

Porter, Michael. "Strategy and the Internet." *Harvard Business Review*, vol. 79, no. 3, March 2001. http://hbswk.hbs.edu/item/2165.html

Rogers, E. M. *Diffusion of Innovations*. New York: Free Press, 1962.

Whitney, Lance. "Smartphone Shipments to Surpass Feature Phones This Year." CNet, June 4, 2013. http://news.cnet.com/8301-1035_3-57587583-94/smartphone-shipments-to-surpass-feature-phones-this-year/

Wiseman, C., and I. C. MacMillan. "Creating Competitive Weapons from Information Systems." *Journal Of Business Strategy*, 5(2) (1984), p. 42.

CPSIA information can be obtained
at www.ICGtesting.com
Printed in the USA
BVOW11s1500160318

510797BV00002B/42/P